PROFILES IN CANADIAN DRAMA
GENERAL EDITOR: GERALDINE C. ANTHONY
Gratien Gélinas
RENATE USMIANI

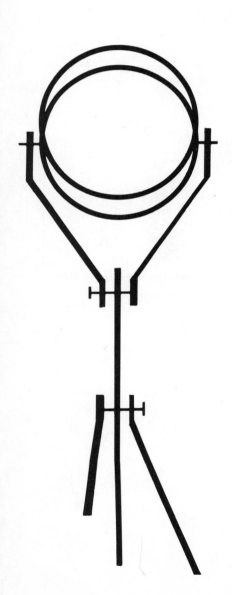

GAGE EDUCATIONAL
PUBLISHING LIMITED

Canadian Cataloguing in Publication Data

Usmiani, Renate, 1931-
  Gratien Gélinas

  (Profiles in Canadian drama)

    Bibliography: p.
    Includes index.
    ISBN 0-7715-5877-5 bd.   ISBN 0-7715-5867-8 pa.
    1. Gélinas, Gratien, 1909-   - Criticism and
    interpretation.   I. Title.   II. Series
    PS8513.E27Z97   C842'.5'4   C76-017216-1
    PQ3919.G35Z97

123456789 GL 84 83 82 81 80 79 78 77

"In Memoriam Leopoldine Herzog, 1890-1975."

Acknowledgements

The author and the publishers wish to thank the following for their co-operation and for their kind permission to quote copyrighted material:

M. Gratien Gélinas for generous assistance to the author in preparation of the manuscript, for permission to publish, in English translation, "Un Théâtre National et Populaire" (which first appeared in *Action Universitaire*, Paris, April 1949), and for permission to quote in English from the unpublished 'Fridolin' sketches.

Clarke, Irwin & Company Limited, Toronto, for permission to quote from Gratien Gélinas: *Bousille and the Just* © 1961, *Tit Coq* © 1967, and *Yesterday the Children Were Dancing* © 1967.

Preface

Profiles in Canadian Drama is a new series of books reflecting a new and exciting phenomenon on the Canadian scene — the development of a sizeable body of solid work which warrants the publication of a series of books devoted solely to Canadian dramatists. While directed primarily to the student of Canadian Literature at the secondary and post-secondary school levels it is also our hope that *Profiles in Canadian Drama* will lead its readers to become not just readers but viewers of Canadian plays.

Gratien Gélinas was one of the first to offer drama as a mirror boldly reflecting French-Canadian life and character. He appeals to both English- and French-Canadian audiences. Logically, then, he is one of the first in this series of profiles. Gélinas has been totally absorbed in theatre for over forty years as dramatist, actor, revue artist, manager, producer, and director. His success derives unquestionably from his ability to reproduce French-Canadian character and idiom on stage with critical openness and wry humor. As an active participant in all areas of Canadian drama, he met the multiform needs of an emerging heterogeneous French-Canadian theatre of radio, film, television and stage with creative ease. In each play he draws in depth one memorable character, a kind of anti-hero. Such was the first and most popular of his characters — Fridolin — the little boy in his old Canadien hockey sweater, speaking rapid colloquial French. Fridolin has become a folk hero in French-Canadian lore. Gélinas is particularly concerned with the integrity of the individual, and his plays follow the radical changes in the evolution of French Canada.

Renate Usmiani's introductory chapter is a unique contribution, offering a brief outline of the history of French-Canadian theatre from colonial times to the present. Her own European background and her study of Comparative Literatures aids her understanding of Gélinas' kind of theatre. In this first book to be published on Gratien Gélinas, Professor Usmiani has read and interpreted the unpublished 'Fridolin' sketches from Gélinas' original manuscripts. Although the remainder of Gélinas' plays have been translated into English, Usmiani has provided a critical comparison of the original French and the English translations; in so doing she has made some telling remarks on the occasional loss of local color, style and meaning. What she has emphasized is the spirit and soul of French Canada as portrayed in the plays and the vivid use Gélinas has made of rural and urban French-Canadian life. The influence of major European playwrights is also referred to. Establishing him thus in the field of drama as a whole, and emphasizing the foundation he laid for a viable French-Canadian theatre for the general public, she has succeeded in providing an in-depth study of this first French-Canadian playwright of note. In an Appendix, the reader can find the text of Gratien Gélinas' Address to the faculty and students of the University of Montreal in 1949 on the occasion of his receiving an honorary doctorate for his contribution to drama. Entitled "A National and Popular Theatre," this address is published here for the first time in English. In it Gélinas gives his rationale for theatre in Canada, and one becomes increasingly aware that Canada has in Gélinas an authentic voice bridging the gap between French and English Canada, not through politics but through art. Though a single voice, he speaks for a bicultural nation.

Geraldine Anthony, S.C.
Mount Saint Vincent University
Halifax, Nova Scotia

Contents

1

Gestation:

The Development of Theatre in French Canada, 1606-1948

On May 22, 1948, at the old Monument National theatre in Montreal, as the final curtain fell on the première performance of Gélinas' first full-length play, Tit-Coq[1], a wave of enthusiasm swept over the audience, a feeling of pride and elation at having been present at that long awaited and longed-for event: the performance of a genuine, French-Canadian drama, a successful play by an author "de chez nous". Critics unanimously claimed the work as the cornerstone upon which a solid independent dramaturgy with an identity of its own could at last be erected. For the first time in the history of French-Canadian theatre, Gélinas had succeeded in putting on the stage a set of characters with whom the audience could identify, and who spoke a language which was their own. Quite instinctively, he had gone to the roots of all genuine theatre: he had tapped the very souls of his fellow countrymen. In so doing, Gélinas finally fulfilled the hopes expressed by Sacha Guitry on a visit to Montreal in 1927. Surveying the aridity of the literary scene in Canada at the time, Guitry had said: "I would like to see Canadian literature, a Canadian theatre develop in your country . . . I would like to see one of you bring on to the stage the Canadian soul . . . ." With Tit-Coq, Gélinas had done exactly that: and for once, general public, critics and academics were unanimous in their instant recognition of that fact (although some of the latter felt called upon to voice their disapproval at the less than classical turns of phrase which make up much of the dialogue). The response aroused by the play was totally out of proportion to its artistic merit, and must be explained in large part by its appeal to the national pride of a people long racked by self-doubt. Thoughtful critics were fully aware of the emotional element inherent in the general acclaim over Tit-Coq. "Shall we ever be able to speak of Tit-Coq objectively?", writes Arthur Laurendeau. Before him, we could applaud only the theatre of foreigners, resulting in a hiatus between art and life; thus, the unanimous joy over Tit-Coq."[2]

"Before him, we could applaud only the theatre of foreigners": the statement correctly reflects the general feeling in 1948 that there simply had been no French-Canadian theatre previous to Gélinas. In objective terms, this is of course not quite true.

In order to see just what sort of a tradition Gélinas had to build upon (obviously, he did not build in a vacuum), we must first of all clearly differentiate between the tradition of theatre, in the sense of theatrical performances, and that of playwriting. And while it is true that scarcely any drama of merit was produced in the three hundred years preceding the appearance of *Tit-Coq*, it is also true that those three hundred years saw an almost unbroken tradition of productions by amateurs, touring groups and, eventually, professionals, a tradition which attests to a genuine interest in, and love for, the theatre on the part of the French-Canadian population — a love all the more remarkable as it had to stand up against continuous disapproval and severe reprimands from a church and clergy ever watchful to keep their flock pure in heart and simple in spirit.

Yet it must be pointed out that the same church which lashed out so vigorously against the theatre contributed immeasurably to keeping the theatrical tradition alive. The seminaries and collèges, all educational institutions run by the church, in fact, remained for some two centuries the only stages where the classics were still performed, as were occasional pieces and edifying works of all kinds, and these performances were open not only to the students and professors of the institution, but often to the general public as well. The church was quite willing to allow the legitimate pleasures of a theatre geared towards education and moral instruction, under the reliable supervision of its own clergy. Trouble arose only when lay groups decided to intervene and run the show on their own.

The uneasy relationship between Church and theatre becomes apparent already in the early history of the theatre in New France, which ended abruptly with a clash between Church and State over a projected performance of Molière's *Tartuffe* in 1694. The French settlers who came to the New World in the 17th century brought with them a love of pageantry and spectacle due no doubt to the all-pervading influence of the court of the Sun King; in their own small way, and with the means at their disposal, they were determined to carry on the tradition of the mother country, which was then at the height of its cultural spendor.

The first spectacle produced in the New World, as early as 1606, was a naval extravaganza, the *Theatre of Neptune*, which was put on by the men of Port Royal to celebrate the return to the fort of the sieur de Poutrincourt, following his expedition to Acadia. The text of this first Canadian "play" was written by a historian, Marc Lescarbot, whose valiant efforts at rhyme would probably not have passed muster at Versailles.

The *Jesuit Relations* provide a wealth of information about subsequent theatrical developments. Performances are popular, not only with the French population, but also with "nos sauvages", the natives, for whose benefit Huron and Algonquin parts are written into the French text. Thus, in 1640, the governor of Quebec, De Montmagny, invited the entire population to join in celebrations honoring the first birthday of the Dauphin, later Louis XV. The celebrations included a solemn procession, a bonfire, and, most importantly, a tragedy composed especially for the occasion. It was the wish of the governor that the play should combine spectacle with a sound moral lesson to the Indians present. This goal was amply fulfilled: in a grand finale, an infidel was chased across the stage by two demons horrible to behold, and uttering dire imprecations in Algonquin, while the jaws of hell opened and the unfortunate sinner was hurtled into the flaming abyss. It is with great satisfaction that the governor reports that this spectacle had all the desired effect upon the terror-stricken natives.

But the repertory of the French régime did not limit itself to spectacle and occasional pieces. As early as 1646, only ten years after the Paris première, Corneille's *Cid* was performed in Quebec, in one of the chambers of the Magasin des Cent Associés, to a mixed audience of laymen, Jesuits and natives. The following years see a series of performances, ranging from Corneille, Racine and Molière to liturgical pageants, Passion plays, and local productions in a mixture of languages: French, Huron and Algonquin. The *Tartuffe* scandal of 1694 eventually put an end to all this theatrical levity. Like many simple incidents, it had far-reaching consequences. *Tartuffe* did not reappear on the French-Canadian stage for another two hundred years.

The idea of staging *Tartuffe* came from the governor of the city, Frontenac, who put a certain lieutenant de Mareuil in charge of the production. When news of these impious plans reached Bishop de Saint-Vallier, he immediately enjoined the governor to cease and desist and threatened his lieutenant with excommunication. As a serious crisis between ecclesiastical and civil authorities seemed imminent, both sides chose the way of diplomacy. His Grace offered the governor the considerable sum of one hundred pistoles in token of his appreciation, and Frontenac cancelled the play. This unsavory affair caused some raised eyebrows at the court, and put an abrupt end to the career of poor de Mareuil.

This incident should not be looked upon as an example of colonial narrow-mindedness, but rather as a reflection of the contemporary intellectual climate in France itself. For the 17th century in France is not only the Golden Age of Corneille, Racine and Molière. The end of the century also marks the violent dispute known as the *querelle du théâtre*, the battle of the theatre, instigated by the Jansenists and spear-headed by Bossuet, Bishop of Condom, theologian, and tutor to the Dauphin. The career of Racine himself illustrates the spiritual crisis of the time: a symbol of that crisis, he moved from the puritan atmosphere of his Jansenist school to the glamour of theatre and court life—and back again, a penitent. It was exactly in 1694, the year of the *Tartuffe* scandal in Quebec, that Bossuet published his major attack against the theatre in his *Reflections on the Theatre*. His arguments can be reduced to three main points, all subsequently adopted by the clergy in their anti-theatre campaigns:

1. Since it is the function of theatre to please, it must necessarily appeal to the passions. (Plato's chief anti-theater argument in the *Republic*, and already successfully countered by Aristotle!)
2. Contemporary theatre does, in fact, afford us copious instances of brutal passions shown on the stage, and the examples cited are Corneille, Racine, and Molière.
3. A long tradition of Church Fathers attests to the wisdom of the Church in opposing this type of entertainment.

The effect of these arguments was rapidly diminished in France, due to the new liberal trends of 18th century Enlightnment. Canada, however, did not undergo a similar development, so that the grip of ecclesiastical censure upon the theatre remained unbroken for another two hundred years. Numerous edicts and pastoral letters attest to the bitterness with which the church attacked any sign of secular theatrical life. Here is a brief sampling, from the diocesan archives, from the late 17th up to the 20th century:

In 1699 in the wake of the *Tartuffe scandal*, Bishop de Saint-Vallier had declared it a "grave sin" to attend any theatrical performance. A hundred years later, the same warnings were still being reiterated by the clergy, notably by the Rev. Joseph-Octave Plessis (1763-1825), curé and later bishop of Quebec. According to his biographer, the Rev. J.B.A. Ferland[3], Mgr. Plessis was particularly zealous in his attempts to suppress any form of frivolous activity which might constitute a threat to the Christian virtues of his flock, especially the young people; he was wont to quote in this connection the remark of Saint Francis de Sales to the effect that such "unbecoming distractions are usually dangerous; they interfere with the spirit of devotion, dampen the spirit of charity, and awaken a thousand evil emotions." However, by the end of the century, the press was already beginning to protest against the excessive puritanical zeal of the clergy in their condemnation of the theatre. And in the 19th century, the church found herself confronted with an enemy considerably more dangerous than the homegrown amateur performances against which she had previously directed her invectives. Professional touring companies had begun to make their appearance, to the delight of the local population and the dismay of their spiritual guardians. Bishop de Bourget saw fit to issue the following pastoral letter when troupes from New York began to draw crowds to a local theater: "For some time, companies of actors and actresses follow each other without interruption in our city, and offer in one of our theatres the spectacle of the most revolting immoralities . . . . The nudity of the actresses would make an honest pagan blush . . . . Scandalous games, criminal dances, grossest indecency are the customary fare which these buffoons offer their audience.

"It is in this den of all the vices that the crimes are committed which compromise the reputation of even the most respectable families, and the peace and prosperity of our citizens. For it is there that mad expenses are incurred to satisfy sensuality and gluttony. It is there that the evil passions are fanned which fill the houses of prostitution. It is there that fabulous sums are squandered, giving proof that one is always rich when it comes to pleasure, while claiming to be poor when it comes to charity. There, money obtained from unsuspecting parents, masters or employers is thrown away madly. There, the noble feelings which link children to their parents are lost. There, these unhappy children learn to despise those to whom they owe their life, to sadden them by their disobedience, and, by a necessary logic, bring upon their heads all the maledictions which are in store for those who do not honor father and mother. . . ."

Just a few months later, Bishop Taschereau was to compose a similar epistle on the occasion of a performance by another New York troupe in Quebec: "Our pastoral duty obliges Us, Our Very Dear Brethren, to raise Our voice today to put you on your guard against a most serious danger which threatens the welfare of your souls. A numerous troupe of foreign performers has announced their intention of giving a series of shows here in the course of next week. We have learned from a most reliable source that these shows violate morality and the most elementary decency to an outrageous degree . . . Should Our counsels not suffice to turn you away from this danger, We do not hesitate to use the authority invested in Us. We absolutely forbid you to attend these theatrical performances."

The battle continues well into the 20th century, the best known cause célèbre being Sarah Bernhardt's visit to Montreal and Quebec in 1905. The archbishop of Montreal, Mgr. Bruchési, as well as Mgr. Bégin, Archbishop of Quebec, took objection to the repertoire which the great actress had decided to bring to Canada, especially Sardou's *La Sorcière*, which was considered offensive to Catholics. This attitude drew the anger of Sarah. In a news conference on December 5, 1905, she made a number of highly uncomplimentary remarks about the country, its people, and the absence of culture; culminating in a bitter attack on the Canadian clergy. When one of the journalists pointed out that the clergy had, after all, done a good deal for French Canadians, the great Sarah snorted disdainfully: "Yes, I suppose — you do owe them this progress in reverse which makes you seem like Turks."

Even from a strictly theatrical point of view, Sarah's total condemnation of the Canadian clergy was not fully justified. They might have considered the theatre a "den of all the vices", but this did not prevent the tradition of productions of clasical plays and religious pageants in the seminaries and collèges to continue unbroken well into the twentieth century, providing a much-needed counterweight to the fluff favored by most of the other amateur groups. And it is only fair to state at this point that the first respectable amateur and eventually, professional, troupe in French Canada grew out of just such a school setting, P. Emile Legault's Compagnons de Saint Laurent, about whom more will be said later.

While the Church had exercised a restraining influence on the development of theatre in French Canada, the change-over from French to British rule, ironically enough, brought with it a strong theatrical revival. Even Molière, banned from the Montreal stage since the *Tartuffe* incident, made his reappearance in the late eighteenth century. Again, we must look to Europe for an explanation of this seemingly paradoxical phenomenon. And in eighteenth century Europe, to be an educated person was tantamount to being at least a francophile if not a gallomaniac. It is the age of total French hegemony in the realm of arts, letters, fashion and *savoir-vivre* in general. French was spoken in every upper-class household; Voltaire could afford to be rude to Frederick the Great at the king's own table, and in Montreal, the conquerors found it necessary to use the language of the conquered if they wanted to appear cultured. The governors of the period (Murray, Carleton, Haldimand, Prevost) spoke flawless French, as did most of the British officers in Montreal. In London, David Garrick, the darling of the British stage, had done much to awaken a taste for the French classics in the local audiences. French companies visiting London may have been booed by the populace on occasion, but they were invariably idolized by the aristocracy. In view of all this, it is not surprising that French plays should feature prominently among the entertainments enjoyed by the British officers and their ladies, even in such remote outposts as Montreal and Quebec. Needless to say, the acting was done by the men exclusively, contemporary etiquette making it quite unthinkable for a respectable lady to appear on stage.

Among the French population, the tradition of theatre was kept only flickeringly alive through the eighteenth and nineteenth centuries. Little documentation is available on the numerous amateur groups which formed and dissolved with predictable regularity. Many factors, most important, probably, the political, contributed to this virtual standstill. With the end of the French régime, there began for the French-speaking population of Canada a period when it was felt that all the energies of the nation must go into simply resisting the enormous anglophone pressures by which French Canadians felt themselves surrounded, and to retain—somehow—a semblance of national identity. This basic concern has been summed up in the *résistance/survivance* (resistance/survival) formula by which critics of the French-Canadian cultural scene are still obsessed today.

The changed political situation brought with it yet another difficulty for the theatre. Would-be producers now found themselves up against, not only the authority of the church but that of the state as well. French amateur groups were often viewed by the authorities with a great deal of suspicion, as potential instigators of rebellion. Thus, when a Quebec company known as the Société d'Amateurs planned a performance of Voltaire's *La mort de César*, in 1839, Lord Thompson was warned by his agents to keep a close eye on the proceedings, which appeared highly suspicious. Caught between the reprobations of Mother Church on the one hand, and close supervision from Her Majesty's Government on the other, it was a miracle that theatre managed to survive at all in French Canada. But survive it did, with even a few feeble attempts at producing an original dramaturgy.

With the popularity of amateur productions undiminished, and the increased stimulation provided by touring companies from abroad, play-writing became a favorite pastime. Members of all the professions tried their hand at it: lawyers, doctors, even the Hon. F. G. Marchand, Premier of the province, who contributed four comedies to the repertoire. Most prolific, of course, were the priests and members of religious orders who held teaching positions, and who considered it part of their work to contribute texts (of the edifying variety, of course) for dramatic performances in their institutions. Needless to say, all of this dramatic production has been mercifully forgotten since, but its sheer bulk attests to the continuing interest in theatre in French Canada.

Some of the playwriting was done by professional authors, men who have since gained a solid reputation as poets or novelists. However, sad to report, their excursions into the field of drama proved hardly more successful than those of their amateur colleagues. An exception could perhaps be made for Joseph Quesnel, a native of Saint-Malo, France, who established himself in Canada and whose comedies, and especially his operetta, *Colas et Colinette*, first performed in Montreal in 1790, became great favorites. So great was Quesnel's success in the theatre that he felt emboldened to produce an *ars poetica* of his very own in 1905, thus linking himself, with an admirable show of immodesty, to the tradition of Aristotle, Horace and Boileau.

Well-known Canadian writers who contributed to the stage during this period were Antoine Gérin-Lajoie, Louis Fréchette and Pamphile LeMay. Gérin-Lajoie, whose novels of manners such as *Jean Rivard* became extremely popular, produced a three-act verse tragedy, *Le jeune Latour*, while still a student at the Séminaire de Nicolet. It is a play obviously patterned after Corneille and attests to the young man's patriotic idealism as well as to the high standards of classical instruction given at the séminaire.

Louis Fréchette, the poet, was doubly unlucky in his dramatic attempts. None of the four plays he produced (*Felix Outré, Le retour de l'exilé, Veronica* and *Papineau*) turned out to be of high quality, and one of them, *Veronica*, involved him in a most unpleasant plagiarism scandal over his use of material provided by a French collaborator. Pamphile LeMay, the poet whose (unfulfilled) life's ambition it had been to produce the great national epic of Canada also contributed three comedies, none of which has survived on stage.

As the above examples show, historical and patriotic subjects were much favored by both amateur and professional writers. Great episodes of Canadian history, such as the battle of the Plains of Abraham, the life stories of Canadian hero figures like Dollard or Riel, and, of course, the courage and devotion of the Christian missionary bringing the true faith to a hostile people gave the authors ample scope with which to uplift and inspire their audiences. Even the more frivolous type of plays, the much-beloved melodramas of the period, never failed to point out a moral. Unerringly, the writer would mete out poetic justice, with goodness finding its just reward and the villain of the piece duly punished at the end. In the early part of the twentieth century, rural idylls also became popular on stage, with writers like Leopold Houlé providing idealized, romanticised tableaux of country life for eager city audiences.

Although amateur performances remained popular throughout, attendance at the plays was often fraught with certain practical difficulties for the theatre-lover of the eighteenth and nineteenth centuries — especially if that person happened to be female. Safety on the streets presented a very real problem, which was partly solved by shows opening at six, so that performances would usually be over by nine o'clock. Even so, respectable ladies, much as they enjoyed the performances, hesitated to be seen in a theatre. To overcome these inhibitions (often implanted by a concerned father confessor), the companies would include in their advertisement of the play a statement to the effect that there was nothing in this performance to offend good taste and morals. Often they went even further to assure the public of the unquestionable respectability of their offerings. An announcement by the Amateurs Canadiens, published in the Montreal paper, *Le Spectateur*, in January, 1817, concludes with the following: "... they (the Amateurs Canadiens) assure the gentlemen and ladies of the city that they will admit only decent and respectable persons; five or six choice benches will be reserved for the ladies and those who accompany them . . . . " Even so, one can imagine the pleasure-loving ladies of Montreal and Quebec casting furtive glances up at their neighbor's window as they try to remain unnoticed returning from a theatre at the disreputable hour of nine p.m!

Even more perhaps than the persistent amateur efforts, visits from professional touring companies gave a real impetus to the development of theatrical life in French Canada. Both English and French companies visited Montreal, usually as part of a North American tour. The best of them provided our theatrically unsophisticated society with two significant factors: an insight into the standards and possibilities of solid professionalism, and definite goals at which to aim. Without the influence of these touring companies and their cultural pollination of the Canadian scene, the development of first-rate professional theatre which took place in Montreal from the 1940's on would have been unthinkable.

Of all the foreign tours, the visits of Sarah Bernhardt to Canada were the most interesting and most colorful. The great actress appeared in Montreal six times between 1880 and 1905. Like theatre itself, of which she had become a symbol, she was made to experience the full ambiguity of the love/hate relationship typical of this country: idolized by some and rudely condemned by others, she was always left confused, and often petulant. A truly royal welcome awaited her on her first visit: a special railroad car had been dispatched to convey her from St. Albans, Vermont, to Montreal, a trip on which she was accompanied by a number of high dignitaries, including the mayor of Montreal and Louis Fréchette, who had composed a special poem to greet her upon her arrival. Montreal society was waiting eagerly for the great actress, who, they hoped, would give them a sampling of her most famous roles — Chimène, in Corneille's *Cid*, or perhaps Racine's *Phaedra*. Instead, Sarah's managers announced a repertory which caused disappointment among the theatre lovers, and indignation among the clergy. On the billboards appeared *Adrienne Lecouvreur*, of Scribe, Meilhac and Halévy's *Froufrou,* and *Hernani,* of Victor Hugo: a playbill which was interpreted as an insult to the Canadian audience. And the general population joined the outcry of the clergy when it was discovered that Sarah was actually planning to give a performance on Christmas Day — a day traditionally given over to religious observance and strictly family celebration. For once, the newspapers were pleased to publish a letter of protest by the Archbishop, the Most Reverend Edouard Fabre, in which he condemned *Adrienne Lecouvreur* as "an immoral play by its very principles, a sad lesson for Christian families." The critic of *La Minerve* expressed the general disappointment when he wrote "we regret that such a great talent should not be put to use in plays more in keeping with our concepts of the great and the beautiful . . . . " The actress herself came up with some half-hearted apologies, blaming the unfortunate choices on her managers who, she said, had not properly informed her as to the tastes of the North American public. However, she did not appear overly dismayed at the criticism which had been raised against her, and for good reasons: her fans were acclaiming her nightly and, after her first performance, had even unharnessed her horses and personally pulled her carriage in a triumphant procession from the theatre to her hotel.

This first visit was to set the pattern for all the subsequent ones: her choice of plays never failed to arouse the ire of the clergy, while her personal magnetism and the superb quality of her acting continued to ensure her the unfailing loyalty and devotion of her admirers. Her high-handed ways antagonized the press, and this antagonism came to a climax in the unfortunate newspaper interview of 1905, which drove Sarah to express some highly negative views about Canada. As a result of this interview, Sarah was booed and pelted with rotten eggs in Quebec, subsequently received with apologies by Sir Wilfrid Laurier in Ottawa, and eventually returned to France, no doubt as mystified as ever about the strange ways of the New World.

The early part of the twentieth century represented a fallow period for theatre in French Canada. It is true that with the growth of the cities, some commercial theatrical ventures had begun, but these theatres catered largely to visiting companies. What plays they produced were in the nature of melodrama or else the ever-popular froth of boulevard comedy. Amateur groups were still active; in fact, they could be found everywhere, even in the smaller communities. But the work they produced was totally out of touch with contemporary trends in Europe. While the early twentieth century on the continent was a period of artistic upheaval, a period of revolution in all the arts, the Canadian stage showed no sign whatsoever of an awareness of all the manifold types of experimentation, in playwriting, in production style, in design, audience participation, and every other conceivable aspect of theatre arts then being carried out in Europe.

This lethargic situation was to change drastically around 1940, due mainly to two major contributions: the work of the Rev. Father Emile Legault, founder of the Compagnons, and the efforts of Radio-Canada. Under these two influences, theatre in French Canada took on a totally new direction.

Father Emile Legault, a member of the Congregation of the Holy Cross, had long been interested in theatre. As a professor at the Collège de Saint Laurent, in a Montreal suburb, he had succeeded in interesting his superiors in his student performances — so much so that he was given a scholarship to study theatre in France under Henri Ghéon, the great champion of Christian revival in the theatre. Father Legault, however, had a sufficiently wide vision of his field to go beyond his original mandate. As well as studying with Ghéon, he worked with Jouvet and Barrault, familiarized himself with the theories of Gordon Craig, and generally expanded his view of theatre, especially of the modern theatre. Returning to Montreal, in 1937, he founded a company of his own, the Compagnons de Saint-Laurent, made up of students. With them, he began to experiment on the basis of his own intuitions and the lessons he had learned during his stay in France. The repertory of the company remained traditional: *Athala, Polyeucte, Britannicus*—the usual playbill of the classical collège. But audiences and critics soon began to notice that there was something about the performances at the Collège de Saint-Laurent which set them apart from run-of-the-mill school plays. Within a short time, Father Legault's group achieved noticeable improvements in both acting and staging. The young actors no longer declaimed with the exasperating monotony typical of the schoolboy style but made genuine efforts at getting across the musical beauty and poetry of the lines of Corneille. The conventional cardboard and papier-mâché realism of the stage gave way to imaginative and more frankly theatrical sets. All these innovations soon made a stir not only in educational circles, but also among the general public, always eager for good theatre, wherever it may be had. To the delight and surprise of Father Legault and his young actors, crowds began to flock to their performances, until the company found itself forced, in 1942, to move to more spacious and more centrally located quarters: they now played in the auditorium of the Collège de Montreal, in a hall called the Ermitage, which housed 800 seats. In 1945, success pushed them further into the heart of the city. They now played at the large Gesù theatre. This last move marked a definite change in the character of the company: from a schoolboy troupe, they had graduated to semi-professional status, well on their way to full professionalism. From now on, they were known simply as Les Compagnons. Their approach had changed greatly since 1937. The original motto of the company had been: "For faith through art, for art in a spirit of faith". Les Compagnons' original artistic creed had been summed up by Father Legault in the following formula: "a poetic, popular and spiritual theatre, presented with esthetic rigor in a Christian climate".[4] Now Father Legault's concern was no longer with developing a Christian theatre exclusively, but simply with laying the foundations for a professional theatre of high standards. In this he succeeded admirably. He managed to recruit practically all of the able acting talent in Montreal. The young actors and actresses who started their career under Father Legault acquired in his company the experience, the artistic standards and the technical know-how which enabled them later to strike out successfully on their own. Practically every one of the theatrical ventures which were soon to proliferate in Montreal were due to the enthusiasm, initiative and know-how of a former Compagnon. Very subtly, Father Legault had expanded his repertoire, from the original emphasis on classical and religious plays, to extend to world theatre, and particularly, modern theatre. Cocteau, Musset, Obey, Shakespeare, Anouilh appear in his repertoire between 1945 and 1948 — a selection which required a good deal of versatility in both performance and acting. Revolutionary innovations were made: as the success of the Compagnons grew, they performed in both French and English; they took their plays on tour, and in 1947 they boldly performed an original Canadian play, Felix Leclerc's *Maluron*. In spite of their quasi-professional status, the Compagnons were officially considered amateurs (no doubt due to the fact that, at the time, it was impossible to make a living by the theatre alone.) Thus they were able to compete in the Dominion Drama Festival, where they won first prize in 1947. In 1948, they moved into a theatre of their own, the Théâtre des Compagnons. By now fully established as the most important theatre in French Canada, they continued their double orientation, perfecting their interpretation of the classics on the one hand, and bringing an international repertoire to Montreal on the other. In 1950, Father Legault made the final concession to the changes that had taken place since he founded the original collège company: from that date on, his actors' names actually appeared on the programmes, thus ending the humbly anonymous state in which they had performed since the company's inception in 1937. By 1952, the Compagnons could look back with pride on their pioneering achievements. They had brought to Montreal a professional approach to the theatre and a worldwide repertoire; they had built up a well-informed audience of some 15,000 loyal theatregoers; they had spawned two important new theatrical ventures, the Théâtre du Nouveau Monde and the experimental Théâtre-Club. Father Legault, tired and beset by financial difficulties, decided to retire in the knowledge of a job well done. The Théâtre des Compagnons closed its doors; the members of the Company dispersed but continued in a variety of ways to carry on the theatrical mission they had undertaken.

The second important influence on the development, perhaps not so much of theatre, but of a theatrical awareness, in French Canada, was that of Radio-Canada. More so than the anglophone section of the CBC, Radio-Canada realized very early the educational potential of radio, and embarked on a veritable mission to bring the heritage of the French classics, as well as world theatre, to its listeners everywhere. This was, of course, particularly important in the rural areas and in remote settlements, which could scarcely be reached by any means other than those of modern mass communication. The most important series in this connection is "Radio-Collège", which started in 1944. The plays in this series were carefully selected to match the literature studies programs of the educational institutions throughout the province of Quebec. In this way, a totally new dimension could be added to the study of dramatic literature, which suddenly became a living reality, rather than just print arranged on a page. Performances of the plays were supplemented with analyses of difficult passages and discussions to help the young audience understand and visualize the works. Another, less formally educational, series, "Le thèâtre classique, romantique et moderne", had been inaugurated as early as 1941. This series brought a cross section of plays illustrating one particular period or movement to its listeners during each broadcasting season. The result of all these efforts was that, just at the time when good theatre began to become available to Montreal audiences, French Canadians everywhere were being initiated into the joyful mysteries of the theatre, simply by tuning in to their local radio station.

Coming back now to the premiere of Gélinas' *Tit-Coq* in 1948, we can see that the time was ripe for "the first French Canadian play" to make its impact. Theatre was an accomplished fact in Montreal. The growing popularity of radio and cinema might reduce the size of theatre audiences, but it also heightened the public's awareness of things theatrical, and thus served as a positive more than a negative influence. Audiences had reached a certain level of sophistication and were demanding quality, even from a homegrown author, an author "de chez nous". Most important, when *Tit-Coq* first appeared, Gélinas had been known and cherished by Montreal audiences for ten years as 'Fridolin', beloved star of the most popular satirical revue in town.

Notes to Chapter One

1. The original French title of the play is "Tit-Coq", ("Little Rooster"). "Tit-Coq" is also used as title in the published English version, translated by Kenneth Johnstone and Gratien Gélinas. However, the simplified spelling "Ti-Coq" was used for English language productions.

2. Laurendeau, Arthur, "Tit-Coq devenu livre", *Action Nationale*, 36; Sept. 1950.

3. Ferland, J.B.A., Abbe; Mgr. Joseph-Octave Plessis (Quebec; Brousseau, 1878), pp. 29-31.

4. *Cahiers des Compagnons de Saint-Laurent,* I, 1, p. 3.

2

Gélinas:

Towards a 'National' and 'Popular' Theatre

No one had been more surprised at the instant success of the "Fridolin" revues than Gélinas himself. Just a few months after his first historic appearance at the Monument National theatre, he had become a legend in show business, and was thereafter generally referred to as 'Fridolin', rather than Gratien Gélinas. It is interesting to note that he stumbled upon his sure-fire formula for success through a gradual process of trial and error, and, of course, by following his inborn instinct for showmanship, which invariably led him in the right direction. He has since analysed the reasons for his immediate appeal to the audience and formulated the results of this analysis. But at the time, he did not have any clear idea of where he was going.

His secret, it eventually turned out, was simply to create for his public a character in their own image, with whom they could instantly identify. Fridolin is nothing more or less than the Everyman of the Montreal working class district. He speaks the language of the people; he suffers their frustrations; he curses their curses. Because Fridolin is only a youngster, he can get away with practically anything; with the impudence and the full immunity of the ragamuffin he represents, he voices his candid opinions of authorities large and small, making us aware of the ways in which Church and School, City Hall and Parliament Hill affect life in the sidestreets and back alleys of Montreal. As Gélinas discovered in the process of developing both the character and the show, the way to the hearts of his public was simply to hold up to them a mirror of their own lives, and to make them cry a little, and laugh a lot, at what they saw. Gélinas never deviated from the view that the playwright's primary concern must be to entertain. Like Brecht, who shared this view, he never lost sight of his primary goal, even when his work became heavy with satire and social criticism. Perhaps because Gélinas is an actor as well as a playwright, he is particularly aware of the theatre artist's obligation, first and foremost, to entertain his audience. And Gélinas is a born entertainer. From the time he was four years old, theatre was the central interest of his life, even though the circumstances of his early life did not favor such an ambition; in fact, they were so very unfavorable that for many years young Gélinas was quite resigned to the frustrations of a business career, relegating the theatre, his first love, to the rank of a leisure time hobby.

Certainly nothing in Gélinas' early life pointed to a successful career in the theatre. Although by his own admission he was "stung by the bug" at the age of four, he was much too level-headed to plan seriously on a career in show business. To do this in Canada when Gélinas was growing up, one had to be either fully insane or independently wealthy. Gélinas answered to neither description.

He was born into a modest home in the village of Saint-Tite, near Trois-Rivières, Quebec, on December 8, 1909. Being born on the feast of the Immaculate Conception — a holy day of obligation in Catholic Quebec — brought him the privilege of never having to attend school on his birthday. It did mean going to Mass instead, but, as he himself later put it, "a holiday from school is well worth a Mass!" His father, Mathias, came from a farming family in the neighboring parish of Sainte-Flore, and had settled in Saint-Tite to ply his craft of harness maker. Mathias took pride in the fact that he could trace his ancestors back to the first Gélinas to land in the New World, in 1628. Gratien's mother, Geneviève Davidson, French speaking herself, came from mixed Scottish and Irish ancestry (a family background he was later to use for the character of the mother in his play *Yesterday the Children Were Dancing*).

The idyllic setting of Saint-Tite did not remain Gratien's home for long, however. By 1909, automobiles and powered farm machinery were replacing horses more and more on the roads and in the fields, and business was bad for a harness maker. When Gratien was only a few months old, Mathias Gélinas therefore decided to move his family (Gratien had one sister) to Montreal, where he eventually found employment as an insurance agent. From the point of view of Gratien's future career, this move had definite advantages: it enabled the child to benefit from the school system of the big city, which was necessarily far superior to the rural one.

However, he did not grow up only as a city boy. Throughout his school years, every summer vacation was spent in the country, where he alternated between his maternal grandfather's house in Saint-Tite, and an uncle's farm in Sainte-Flore. While Gratien was an extremely quiet and studious child in Montreal, a bookish perfectionist forever struggling to make it to the top of his class in school, he became a different sort of boy altogether in the country. Books and lessons were forgotten, and all summer long he would run wild with his friends and cousins, of whom he had vast numbers, especially in Sainte-Flore. He himself attributes many of the lovable attributes of his Fridolin—the freshness, spontaneity and insouciance — to the experience of these carefree summers in the country, and he is convinced that he would not have been able to create a character of this sort, had his entire life been spent in the restrictive environment of the big city.

It is easy to see his point. Even today, Saint-Tite still exudes some of that idyllic atmosphere of which the memories of happy childhood summers are made. A large village of some five thousand inhabitants, it lies in one of the wide, fertile river valleys typical of the Laurentian landscape. Cattle graze on both sides of the road as one enters the village across a small bridge. Typical French architecture prevails, the houses looking very decorative with their wrought iron staircases winding up to the second floor balconies. Most of the streets are named after saints, with the obligatory rue Notre Dame leading up to the main square. Above a church which appears oversized in relation to the village, two picture-postcard spires glisten in the sunlight. There is a square expanse of lawn where the village youth congregate, and, obviously the pride of Saint-Tite, a circular fountain, in the middle of which stands the statue of a huge horse, painted in rather garish shades of brown and dripping under the sprays of water. The latter objet d'art attests less to the artistic taste of the inhabitants of Sainte-Tite than to their sense of public relations: traditionally the home of much leather craft, Saint-Tite has recently become the site of an annual rodeo to publicise its manufacture of cowboy boots. Other than that, the village is much as it was in the days when Gratien Gélinas and his playmates occupied the village green: two small hotels, rocking chairs for the guests provided outside on the narrow sidewalk, a tavern, some small eating places, and, of course, the ubiquitous drugstore. At the edge of the village, on rue Delisle, one can still see the tiny grey frame house which was the Gélinas home before the family moved to Montreal. It is hardly visible from the street; bushes have overgrown it, and the two small dormer windows lie hidden behind the branches of a big tree.

Saint-Tite, and especially Sainte-Flore, where he had more playmates, were ideal places for a young boy with a lively imagination like Gratien. From the beginning, his boyhood games included theatrics of all kinds. He put on shows which covered the full range of dramatic genres—from monologues and puppet plays to high drama—and never knew the frustration of playing to an empty house, as his relatives and friends invariably provided him with an appreciative and conveniently unsophisticated audience.

As we have said, he had contracted his passion for show business suddenly, the way one contracts a disease, at the tender age of four. At that time, one of Gratien's cousins, Charles Duval, who was studying law in Montreal, came to call on the Gélinas family on a Sunday afternoon. This young man was a master in the then popular art of ''declamation,'' i.e., he could recite, for the pleasure of anyone who cared to listen, an entire repertory of popular poems and short prose pieces. Little Gratien listened in awe while his cousin gave his dramatic performance in the living room, and he would not let Charles stop until he had fully exhausted not only his repertory, but also his vocal chords. That day made an actor of Gratien Gélinas. The following afternoon, his mother discovered the child in a corner of the living room, reciting bits and pieces he remembered from the previous day's declamation and accompanying his efforts with much grandiose gesticulation. It was the beginning of his career as a monologist. He never stopped practicing from that day on, and very soon discovered that his special talent lay in comic recitations, in which he emulated his father, who had a great reputation as a teller of funny stories.

During his subsequent summers in the country, Gratien was able to give free rein to his passion for the theatre. With the help of costumes provided by his aunt in Sainte-Flore, and some very elementary make-up, he would create half a dozen characters, whose monologues entertained his audience — often some thirty relatives and friends — in the village. At his grandfather's house in Saint-Tite, he had the good fortune of inheriting a closet full of theatre accessories which had been used in amateur theatricals long ago. Inspired by these wooden swords, military hats, and wigs, he would invent truly epic spectacles, which were produced with the help of his sister on the boards of his grandfather's sawmill. Also at this time, Gratien was first introduced to professional theatre, when his relatives took him to see a melodrama entitled *Martyre*, which was performed by the Barry-Duquesne company in the market hall of the neighbouring town of Shawinigan. This performance left an indelible impression upon young Gratien. From that moment on, Fred Barry became the boy's hero. Some fifteen years later, that same Fred Barry had become Gélinas' close friend and collaborator!

But playing at theatre was not restricted to the summer vacations. Although a serious and ambitious student, Gratien nevertheless had a tendency to evaluate any educational institution more from the point of view of its theatrical potential than that of its scholastic usefulness. It was thus that he was almost drawn into the religious life. As it happened, one of his uncles, Father Olivier Gélinas of the congregation of the Blessed Sacrament, suggested to the family that Gratien, then twelve years old, be sent to the congregation's boarding school at Terrebonne. The parents were delighted at the suggestion, as their means were modest, and this arrangement would provide their son with an excellent education at an extremely low cost. Gratien was equally enthusiastic at the prospect, as he had heard that theatrical performances were much favored by the good fathers. There was one slight inconvenience, though, which no one at first thought of: this school was really intended for boys who felt a strong religious vocation, and planned to become both priests and members of the congregation. Gratien spent one happy year at Terrebonne, but at the end of that year, the fathers made it very clear to the family that he would be better off at some other school, having discovered quite soon that the boy's true vocation lay in the costume closet rather than in the chapel. And so he moved on to the Collège de Montréal, an institution run by the Sulpicians. He enjoyed the intellectual challenge and the spirit of competition which prevailed in this large school of some six hundred students, as compared to a population of only sixty at Terrebonne. Gratien, intelligent and hard working, usually managed to fulfill his ambition of winning first place in his class. He was especially good in languages. He excelled in French and Latin, and was fascinated by history. On the other hand, he found geography boring, and mathematics difficult. Always a perfectionist, he suffered unending frustration when a study period ended before he could give his work all the detailed attention he would have liked, and he envied his non-boarding colleagues, who could stay up all night if they wanted, in order to complete their homework. This perfectionist spirit remains a characteristic of Gélinas. He works his plays over and over again until he is quite sure that each line and expression is exactly right; in his acting and especially his directing, he shows the same punctilious attention to perfection of detail. He received an excellent classical education at the Collège de Montréal, and he supplemented this formal education with extensive reading on his own — reading which often had to be done clandestinely. While other boys were hiding in the toilets to smoke, Gratien used that same refuge to indulge his passion for books.

In spite of his obvious pleasure in the intellectual stimulation afforded by school, Gratien would hardly have been happy there if he had not also had an opportunity to exercise his other great passion, that for the theatre. The Collège proved an excellent place for a budding young actor, as it boasted an active Drama Society, which, under the direction of one Father Nadeau, put on two major productions a year. Gratien was happily involved in these theatricals from the beginning, starting out in tragic roles, but soon veering in the direction of comedy, where his real talents lay. Gélinas still remembers the incident which first raised in his mind certain doubts as to his vocation as a tragic-heroic actor. In a school play dealing with the persecution of the Christians in ancient Rome, he played the part of the villainous traitor who delivered an innocent young victim to his fate in the lions' den. Having pronounced his final dramatic line with all the required grandiloquence, he turned to leave the stage, expecting from the audience a reaction of horror shrouded in silence. Instead, a loud outburst of laughter accompanied his exit. As he discovered later, his vigorous movement as he turned around to exit had made his short tunic fly up, exposing the bottom part of his anatomy. Like his previous experience with the Fathers of the Blessed Sacrament, this incident again served to set him even more clearly on his course.

Gratien had been happy at the Collège de Montréal. He had hoped to go on to university to study law. However, the depression of 1929 forced him to abandon his studies and look for work. But jobs were scarce in 1929. Eventually, he found employment as a salesman in the yard goods department of Dupuis Frères, a Montreal department store. He stayed there for only one summer, which turned out to be the hardest summer of his life. Hours were from 8:30 a.m. to 6:30 p.m., Monday through Saturday, and the pay amounted to ten dollars a week. In the fall, he managed to find a somewhat better job, in the accounting department of a big insurance company, La Sauvegarde. He was now working in an office, collecting a grand salary of some nineteen dollars weekly, and, most important, he had Saturday afternoons off.

The following years were hectic ones. Monday through Saturday, he was working at La Sauvegarde. Saturday afternoon, he had taken on an extra job as a shoe salesman in a large chain store, bringing in thereby an extra three dollars a week. In the evenings, he attended business courses at the Ecole des Hautes Etudes Commerciales — a training which was to stand him in good stead in his later capacity of theatre administrator. In between, he still found time to court a beautiful young girl, Simone Lalonde, who was to become his wife, and the mother of his six children.

Meanwhile, needless to say, he had not given up his interest in the theatre. Economic necessities had made him realize that this interest could not be more than a hobby; but as a hobby, he was determined to pursue it for the rest of his life. No sooner had he left the Collège de Montréal, than he began to organize an alumni company, the "Troupe des Anciens du Collège de Montréal." The group brought together an assortment of recent graduates, mostly young professionals, and businessmen who shared Gélinas' enthusiasm for the theatre, and, finding that commodity almost non-existent in Montreal, decided to provide it for themselves. Their schedule called for three productions a year, which were given in the auditorium of their alma mater. Their repertory was made up mostly of comedies — which points clearly to the overriding influence of Gélinas in the group. Labiche was the favorite. Although these were no longer schoolboy productions, they still suffered from the usual handicap of the collège plays: there were no females in the cast. Until Father Legault boldly included women among his Compagnons, all such performances were based on plays especially adapted for a cast of young men — which meant a virtual re-writing of the plays. All female parts would be taken out, the lines to be spoken by females put into the mouths of assorted messengers. The method proved especially clumsy in the case of love scenes. The problem there was usually solved by having the lover converse, not with his beloved directly, but with her little brother, who would pop on and off the stage, delivering messages and bringing replies, a system not really conducive to heightening audience interest in the proceedings.

Things were somewhat better at the Montreal Repertory Theatre, which, although not a professional company, already boasted a French and an English section. Gélinas was active in both; his quite limited knowledge of English did not discourage him from tackling a Shakespearean part, and he played Doctor Caius, in *The Merry Wives of Windsor*, with great aplomb, if not with a full understanding of what he was saying.

Although Gélinas, in the early years of his career, was quite resigned to the fact that theatre for him must remain an amateur activity, he actually did earn the occasional five dollar fee for appearances on radio, which he somehow managed to work into his crowded schedule. His capacity to work up to twenty hours a day was a great help during these difficult early periods; later on, it made it possible for him to keep up with the hectic pace of his successful years.

Radio eventually provided Gélinas with the opportunity which marked the beginning of his career as a professional in show business. In 1932, Robert Choquette, already a well-known poet, was commissioned by Radio-Canada to produce the first serial (''radio-roman'') of the network. ''Le Curé de Village'' was to go on the air a quarter hour a day, five days a week. When auditions for the serial were announced, Gélinas decided to present himself. He went home that day with an important part, and the assurance of the fabulous salary of twenty dollars a week. He was now a professional.

It took two more successful experiments, however, before the ever cautious Gélinas made up his mind to leave the insurance company and take the full financial plunge into show business. The first of these was his participation in a satirical revue produced by the two then best known journalists of Montreal, Jean Béraud and Louis Francoeur. The revue, prophetically entitled ''Télévise-moi ça'', was a great success, and the most successful number in it was a series of monologues, written and delivered by Gratien Gélinas. He brought down the house, had to answer three curtain calls, and understood that he had found his proper medium: the dramatic monologue. Things began to move very quickly after his success in ''Télévise-moi ça.'' Soon afterwards, Henri Letondal, artistic director of the cabaret Ici Paris, invited Gélinas to perform a series of monologues. His reputation as a monologist (''a one-man entertainment machine'', as he likes to call himself) was now growing rapidly, and he came to be much in demand by social groups and charitable organizations. His experiences with these events, where he often had to compete with the hoarse shouting from bingo announcers and cotton candy vendors, were not always the happiest, but they did provide him with an opportunity to test his lines and his manner of delivery on an audience, and to perfect his style. By 1937, he decided he was ready at last, and he accepted an offer to run a radio show of his own. With the consent and encouragement of his wife, he gave up his job at La Sauvegarde. Fridolin was about to be born.

The success of the show made it clear to critics and audiences alike that Gélinas had at last found that elusive, magic formula upon which a genuine French-Canadian theatre could be built. John Coulter, who saw the ''Fridolin'' show of 1946, felt that Gélinas was doing for Canada ''what the Abbey Theatre did for Ireland, or the Moscow Art Theatre for Russia''.[1] Surely a hyperbolic statement, but it does contain an element of truth: the character of Fridolin served, as did Gélinas' later plays, to crystallize the consciousness and sense of identity of the people of French Canada.

Gélinas' formula is deceptively simple. He has stated it himself repeatedly since these early days, in newspaper interviews, in his published theatrical credo[2], and, most succinctly, in the acceptance speech he made at the University of Montreal in 1949, upon receiving an honorary doctorate from that institution.[3] The title of the speech, ''A National and Popular Theatre'' sums up the essence of his beliefs: Theatre is by its very nature both ''popular'' and ''national''. In the case of Canada, and especially Quebec, which so far lacks a truly national theatre, and lives in cultural dependency on the former mother country, these criteria are particularly important. Since theatre is practically unknown here, the public should be introduced to it gradually, starting on the popular level. The aim, then, is to ''bring together, in one and the same emotion, the great and the humble, the rich and the poor, the ignorant and the learned . . . ''[4] This goal was magnificently achieved in the ''Fridolin'' revues, which drew to the theatre a mixed crowd of enthusiasts made up from every social and educational stratum of society. And Fridolin miraculously appealed as much to the little man with the lunch pail as to the learned professor sitting next to him. Gélinas' ability to establish such total rapport with his audience reflects his belief that the close relationship between stage and auditorium represents the very essence of theatre. The communion between actors and public should be as close as that of husband and wife at the moment of love. This principle of total union brings us back to the need for a national theatre; for ''how can such a complete union take place in our halls between our own public and an author with a foreign mentality?''[5] On the other hand, Gélinas not only felt sure, but actually proved by the success of his own work, that, as he claims, ''the public will fall head over heels in love with the theatre the day it sees itself on stage, caught in the midst of its own sufferings, its own joys!''[6] With his ''Fridolinons'', Gélinas succeeded in putting before his countrymen a series of shows genuinely national and popular, in both inspiration and language, which perfectly illustrate his dramatic creed. The Fridolin revues certainly achieved this basic purpose — and in the process, contributed to the enjoyment of delight of many thousands over a period of ten years.

Notes to Chapter Two

1. Coulter, John; Theatre Review, ''Fridolinons '46''', *Saturday Night*, Jan. 18., 1947.

2. Gélinas, Gratien, ''Credo of the Comédie Canadienne. (The Faith Behind the 'Little Miracle')'', *Queen's Quarterly*, Spring 1959.

3. Gélinas, Gratien, ''Un théâtre national et populaire'', *Action Universitaire*, April 1949. Cf. Appendix.

4. *Un théâtre national et populaire*, p. 39.

5. *Un théâtre national et populaire*, p. 34.

6. *Credo*, p. 22.

3

A Lesser Hero: Fridolin

Fridolin was born on September 23, 1937, under the auspices of a weekly radio program entitled "Le Carrousel de la gaîté," over station CKAC, Montreal; from 1939 to 1941, the show was entitled "Le train de plaisir". Although the author found it difficult to change over from the monologue style to which he was accustomed, to the dialogue form required by radio, the show was an instant success. Within months, 'Fridolin' became a household word in French Canada. The extent of the show's popularity can best be measured by the fact that, in March 1938, CKAC found it necessary to warn its listeners against the proliferation of "false Fridolins" which had appeared on the air, produced by "unscrupulous imitators" eager to cash in on the general appeal of the show. Gélinas suddenly found himself in the same enviable, if exasperating, situation as the one Cervantes had to cope with after the success of his *Don Quixote*! The historical parallel is interesting, especially because, as we shall see later, the characters of Fridolin and Don Quixote are not without certain basic similarities.

Encouraged by the enthusiastic reception of Fridolin on radio, Gélinas decided, in 1938, to expand the show to the format of a live revue. For two and a half years, the radio and stage shows ran parallel, (a tour-de-force for the author-actor-producer-director!). From 1941 on, Gélinas abandoned the radio show and devoted his energies fully to the revue, which was produced annually until 1946, with a revival in 1956. The stage shows were entitled "Fridolinons", ("Fridolinons '39", "Fridolinons '40", etc), from the theme song of the show, in which the name Fridolin was conjugated like a verb ("il vaut mieux Fridoliner . . . ").

There is an unquestionable evolution in the quality of the texts from the early radio shows to the sketches of the revues. The manuscripts of the first two years especially show a rapid progress in the handling of language, the structuring of the dialogue, and the creation of character. As the author gradually found his style, the amount of "filler material" in the shows decreased, until he achieved the concentration and consistently high quality which marks the best of the revues. But in spite of this necessary groping for a basic style, and the equally necessary gradual sharpening of the artistic tools employed, the essential elements which were to make Fridolin a landmark in the evolution of French Canadian theatre were there from the very start: the characterization of Fridolin himself, and the kind of language employed. Long before the theoretical formulation of his theatrical principles, Gélinas had instinctively created that 'national and popular' theatre which was bound to appeal to a society which was as yet theatreless. The third element which explains the resounding success of the Fridolin shows is Gélinas' total commitment to entertain — a commitment especially important in time of crisis. And we must bear in mind that the Fridolin shows, 1937-1946, cover the most disaster-filled period of the twentieth century. The introduction to the program on February 1, 1939, illustrates exactly the intentions of Gélinas: "Mussolini wants Tunisia; Hitler, the Ukraine; Daladier, airplanes; Chamberlain, peace. But there is a young man who wants only one thing: to make you forget your troubles: that's Fridolin." As time went on, and the revue became more consistently satirical, with serious overtones of social and political criticism, Gélinas never lost sight of this first goal. As Father Legault pointed out when he presented Gélinas to the Royal Society, "You belong to the tradition of Chaplin, Molière and those other moralists who have chosen to purge society of its follies by making it laugh at itself . . . . "

With Fridolin, Gélinas created a character with whom his contemporaries could identify, in idiom and outlook. At the same time, because of Fridolin's youthfulness and low social standing, there was retained the distance which is necessary to make satire effective, but not painful. The language of the Fridolin shows is fully and unashamedly colloquial French Canadian, without, however, becoming *joual*. While creating the illusion of total realism, it is of course a carefully created dramatic idiom: as Gélinas points out, a simple transferring of the language of the streets onto the stage will not achieve an effect of realism; a successful dramatic idiom requires a great deal of "choice" and "elaboration". The characters of the Fridolin shows speak a French heavily interspersed with English expressions — "tu parles d'une bad luck!"; "heu! on a eu un fun!"; "on va le smacker" — anglicisms of which they are fully unaware. In fact, Gélinas uses this particular aspect of French-Canadian parlance, the unconscious use of English expressions, as the object of satire in one of the early episodes, when he has Fridolin comment sadly on his limited knowledge of the English language, and his lack of motivation for acquiring it, when one has such good French expressions at one's disposal, anyway: how, for instance, would one ever say "soda" in English, or "slingshot", Fridolin's favorite toy? He is much amazed, and not fully convinced, when he learns that these words actually are English, and not French at all. On the other hand, there is no question that the language spoken in Fridolin's part of Montreal is totally different from classical or international French: it is indeed a national idiom, and not the language of a far off mother country. The distinction is emphasized again in one of the episodes, when Gélinas has Fridolin return from a trip to Paris and heave a sigh of relief at the prospect of being able again at last to speak French in the way which to him comes naturally: "to go around in shirtsleeves, phonetically speaking". Gélinas is also fully aware of the important part played by cursing in a language which purports to be popular. In a strongly Catholic society like that of Quebec, this type of expression tends to be taken from the context of religion and liturgy, thus verging on the blasphemous. In the radio shows, this aspect of the language had to be carefully censored because of the prevailing taboos of the mass medium. On stage, Gélinas took increasing liberties, especially in those sketches which no longer featured the child Fridolin as the central character, but depicted a naturalistic scene of everyday life among the lower classes. Even Fridolin's favorite expression, "eh, souffrance" on the radio, is intensified to "maudite souffrance" in the revue. By trial and error, forever keeping a close tab on audience reactions and adjusting his style accordingly, Gélinas eventually developed the effective dramatic idiom which enabled him to move on from short sketches to full-length drama.

The first and most important element in the success of the shows was of course the character of Fridolin, always played by Gélinas himself. Fridolin was originally conceived as a vehicle for dramatic monologue. For the radio show, the monologue form had to give way to dialogue, with Fridolin flanked by two side-kicks in the style of the American Jack Benny show. After some initial difficulty with this form, Gélinas discovered that it allowed him to expand into small episodes and sketches, which eventually grew into complete plays. The basic character of Fridolin was never changed. From the beginning, he was conceived of as a young boy, some fourteen or fifteen years old, of unprepossessing appearance, but with an endearing personality. Fridolin is small for his age—so puny, in fact, that at one point he embarks on an exercise program (predictably unsuccessful) in order to come closer to his hero, Tarzan. Fridolin's outfit did not change throughout the years. A typical French-Canadian boy, he wears short pants, with suspenders that are forever slipping off, a tri-color hockey sweater, a pair of unruly knee socks, and he carries his slingshot with him wherever he goes. Fridolin is a child of the slum district of East Montreal. "La cour", the dingy yardspace between the tenements where he lives, is his kingdom and the center of his operations: for Fridolin commands the loyalties of a colorful *bande*, a gang of boys and girls whom he leads in a life of high adventure among the back alleys and garbage cans.

The secret of Fridolin's success lies largely in the ability of the author to combine humor and pathos in the same character: a combination which was to reappear later in both *Tit-Coq* and *Bousille and the Just*. First and foremost, the "Fridolinons" are humorous shows, providing their audiences with laughter and light entertainment through the amusing antics of young Fridolin, but as in all good comedy, there is a constant awareness of the underlying sad and even tragic realities. Fridolin and his gang have endless fun in their yards filled with discarded treasure, but we are never allowed to forget the raw poverty of their existence. Gélinas makes us laugh at the sight of Fridolin's comic disappointment when he finds a pair of long underwear under the Christmas tree, instead of the bicycle he had hoped for, but deep down we know very well that tears would be more appropriate. It is highly amusing to watch the group of boys and girls drooling over a set of cook books, trying to recreate in their imaginations gourmet treats they will never know, but the hilarity which the scene evokes is mixed with uneasiness.

What makes the charm of Fridolin is his invincible optimism in the face of difficulties of which he is quite aware. A whole popular philosophy of life, with its courage and resignation, is contained in Fridolin's favorite exclamation, "eh, souffrance!" His full awareness of the realities of existence is made clear in one of the episodes when he decides to write an autobiography with the telling title "Ma vie, cette garce", "My Life, That Bitch." Gélinas makes it clear from the outset that Fridolin's life is fraught with enormous hardships and difficulties. The redeeming feature, however, and the one which makes him so very lovable, is his determination to keep on trying in the face of continuous defeat and disappointment. From this point of view, Fridolin could be seen as a most effective symbol of French Canadian society, a concrete embodiment of that quality of *survivance* under most adverse and difficult circumstances in which French Canadians pride themselves. Fridolin never gives up. Forced to live in a sordid, depressing and often hopeless reality, he escapes by creating for himself a fictional dream world in which all problems are resolved equitably, and a boy gets to enjoy all the sodas and sundaes he can eat. As in *Don Quixote*, the basic theme underlying all the Fridolin episodes is that of the discrepancy between the ideal and the real. Like Don Quixote, Fridolin on his own small scale, attempts to build a world according to his dream. Like Don Quixote, he goes down in defeat whenever dream and reality clash; but he comes back, full of hope, to try again in the next episode.

The pathos of Fridolin's life is set from the very beginning in the radio shows, through an episode which tells of his bastard origin and through the recurrent disappointments in his attempts to win for himself the love of a pretty girl, Anzelma. The episode in which Gélinas has Fridolin tell, quite casually, of how he came to acquire his particular set of parents reveals the general sociological background of the show; it is also interesting because it shows Gélinas' preoccupation, as early as 1938, with the bastard theme, which was to become the focal point of *Tit-Coq*. With no apparent show of emotion, Fridolin informs his chums that he, instead of their own son, was brought home one day by his present parents, his father having decided to take home the best among the baby carriages parked in front of the store where they were shopping. The ups and downs of Fridolin's love story with the beauteous Anzelma also provide humor tinged with bitterness. Ideal and real clash in constant comic juxtaposition: Fridolin sends flowers to the lady (the ideal gesture of the swain in love), but reaps only insults in return (Anzelma fails to see the symbolic significance of his bouquet of dandelions); he threatens to commit suicide, the approved romantic act of the rejected lover, but then decides against such a course of action, when he realistically understands that there would be little point in it for him, unless he could at least watch Anzelma's face as she is given the tragic news.

The humor in the radio shows goes all the way from ordinary puns to situation comedy, incongruity and satire. There is an occasional touch of absurd reasoning, such as the New Year's episode when Fridolin has his entire gang worried about the possibility of being swallowed up in the void between the two years. "What if the old year runs out and the new one fails to arrive on time?" The satire is generally milder than in the later stage shows. There is already in the radio shows a certain amount of political satire, with "notre Maurice"[2] the prime target. The municipal government of Montreal comes in for its share of the fun, such as when Fridolin dispatches a delegation of boys to thank the mayor for his negligence about snow removal, which has turned the city streets into a veritable paradise for sledding and building snow forts. But the full force of Gélinas' dramatic and satirical talent did not appear until Fridolin was transferred to the stage of the large Monument National theatre in 1938.

The character of Fridolin, always played by Gélinas in the costume which became traditional, remained central to the revue, even though the format was expanded considerably. The two and a half to three hour revue was composed of music, ballet, and satirical sketches, with Fridolin acting as general Master of Ceremonies for the show and also taking the lead in many of the sketches. In spite of the expanded format, Gélinas was careful to retain the generally Canadian and specifically French-Canadian character of the show. Even in the musical numbers, as well as the dances, he managed to stay clear of the temptation to use jazz or any other American popular music; instead, the musical and dance numbers of "Fridolinons" were original creations inspired by Canadian folklore. The dramatic sketches fall roughly into two categories: mini-plays of domestic realism, which give a naturalistic and satirical slice of life from the everyday affairs of the ordinary French Canadian, and satires on Canadian public affairs. The former eventually lead up to full-length plays; ("Le retour du conscrit", "The Conscript's Return", 1946, can really be considered the first version of *Tit-Coq*); the latter belong more specifically to the revue style. The realistic sketches are already independent playlets which do not feature Fridolin. In the satirical pieces, on the other hand, Fridolin invariably appears in a key role, making full use of the immunity he enjoys, being a "mere child".

The satirical sketches range in theme from international to national to specifically French-Canadian affairs. Even in those sketches which focus more particularly on world events, the emphasis is always on how these events affect the Canadian situation. In each one of the "Fridolinons", the great drama of World War II is felt only as a presence, a background — but never as an immediate reality. Like the authors of regional novels, Gélinas remains in the home environment at all times, well aware of the developments outside, but basically interested only in how these developments affect life chez nous. An excellent example in point is furnished by Gélinas' satirical take-off on the 1944 Quebec conference, when Canada played host to Winston Churchill and Franklin D. Roosevelt, and a new charter was drawn up. In the 1944 edition of the revue, the author inserted a sketch, "by" and with Fridolin, entitled "Si j'étais King" ("If I Were King")—a discreet pun on the name of the Canadian Prime Minister, Mackenzie King — in which he mercilessly exposes the exploitation and subordination of Canada at the hands of the great powers. The conference is treated rather disrespectfully as the subject matter for an operetta with Fridolin taking the main part, that of King I, ruler of the "Gogoths". During a lighthearted first scene in which Fridolin re-enacts the famous seventeenth century *lever du roi* (the king's ceremonial rising from bed), we learn that preparations are under way for a big conference which will bring Uncle Samuel, President of the "Yankeegoths", as well as John Bouboule, Prime Minister of the "Anglogoths," to the court of His Majesty King I; the purpose of the conference being to set down in a charter the principles which are to ensure a better life for the era of peace impending after the expected defeat of the obnoxious "Nazigoths." The illustrious visitors arrive, but they show a disconcerting unwillingness to work (they have brought fishing gear and golf clubs) as well as total disregard for their host, who has, after all, summoned all the resources of his modest country (including a solitary ballerina) to welcome them in style. Uncle Samuel in particular gives rise to grave misapprehension from the moment of his arrival, as he looks around him and comments "You have a beautiful big country all right, but are you sure it really belongs to you?" As the day goes on, it becomes increasingly clear that the two guests hold their host in total disdain: every time he pops up to make a speech, they push him back down onto his chair; when they pose for the press, they push him out of the picture; and at the banquet, they divide the beautiful cake that is brought in among themselves, while not even a crumb goes to poor King I. There is some bitter satire on the economic implications of the war contracts. While John and Samuel are careful to retain their ability to produce consumer goods so that they will be ready for a return to peacetime economy, an all-out war effort is demanded of Canadians, who will thus be unable to compete with the bigger powers. The historical accuracy of this type of accusation could be questioned, but there is no doubt whatsoever that it furthered the cause of Canadian nationalism! Fridolin/King's final speech combines the usual wartime clichés about victory with heavy satire on the precarious state of Canadian unity: "King: Yes, let us fight for the defense of our flag. (John whispers something in his ear) Excuse me, we haven't got a flag . . . . In that case, let us fight for national unity. (Samuel whispers someting in his ear) Not that either? Gee . . . we are in a mess . . . Oh well, let us just fight . . . we'll see later . . . . '' In the finale to the operetta, the orchestra varies the Fridolin song so as to vaguely resemble "God Save The King".

The same concern about the lack of national unity, brought home at once realistically and symbolically by the non-existence of a Canadian flag, runs through all the sketches dealing with Canadian affairs. A particularly effective sketch on this theme was produced as part of the 1942 revue, which re-enacts the founding of Montreal in the seventeenth century, this time by Fridolin. This particular sketch is interesting not only as satire but also from the point of view of dramatic technique, as it cuts back and forth in time between the seventeenth and twentieth centuries. This sketch starts out with Fridolin studiously going through history tomes in the library of the National Archives when he makes a momentous discovery: contrary to popular belief, Montreal was not founded by Maisonneuve at all, but by an ancester of Fridolin, Dieumegarde La Fronde, Sieur de Fridolin, along with a company of actors, who preceded the Sieur de Maisonneuve by several days. Fridolin is not overly surprised that this important historical fact should have escaped notice until now: "After all, French Canadians read so very little!" He thereupon proceeds to re-enact the founding of the city. His greatest difficulty lies in convincing the native population of the advantages of the civilized life which comes with official founding. The Indians of Montreal point to the example of Quebec, which has already been founded for some thirty years, and things there do not seem very encouraging. But Fridolin brushes away their fears with a confident "Oh, well, I see your point, but then, as a founder, old Samuel didn't have my twist (sic)." The whole company then sings the praises of civilization in a series of couplets designed to convince the innocent savages of the advantages of taxes, political corruption, modern weaponry and such innovations as hot dogs and hamburgers — not to mention "Pipi-Cola" and "Caca-Cola". The natives are unable to resist these enticements to be so pleasantly poisoned and agree to the founding of the city. A charter is then drawn up, which enumerates all the contemporary grievances of the French-Canadian population of Montreal (corruption in politics and in the police force, the high cost of electricity furnished by the "Hochelaga Tight, Teat and Tower Co., etc). As to population arrangements, "all the people with money will live in the West". The new city is to be provided with elaborate sports facilities, but not a theatre. Eventually, Fridolin actually brings in a flag for the new community. The flag contains a symbol for each part of the Province of Quebec, as well as a central "dog and cat fight, to symbolize national unity."

Occasionally, Gélinas' satire is directed at the internal politics of French

Canada. One of the numbers of ''Fridolinons '45'' directs its satire against the unsuccessful Bloc Populaire Party, conveniently renamed Flop Populaire by Fridolin, who has decided to go into politics in this particular sketch. As leader of a new party, Fridolin also takes issue with the current family allowance controversy, on which he decides to address English-speaking voters in their own language. The resulting speech gives a good illustration of Gélinas' ability to capture the French Canadians' unconscious mixing of the two languages, regardless of which of the two they claim to be speaking at the moment: ''Permettez-moi de dire quelques mots . . . dans la langue de Tchékspire, du colonel Drew et du Pasteur Shields . . . Dear compatriots Blokes . . . I read in the different gazettes that you don't like the new law about allocations familiales . . . I comprehend your opposition to that law . . . You have reason . . . Parce que . . . heu, because us, French pea soups, we have big families of twenty-five children minimum . . . So we receive from the gouvernement big poches of money . . . And you, you have many dogs but small families of two children, one or not at all pantoute . . . you will have a small poche, flat, flat! So I have an idea: if you vote for us and when we are at the pouvoir, you can put on your rapport the dogs together avec the children . . . So you will have a big poche like us! . . . ''

Of all the Fridolin revues, the one of 1945 was probably the most successful; it also contains Gélinas' most serious criticism of French-Canadian society. In ''The Edifying Life of Jean Baptiste Laframboise'', he points out the tragic waste of talent and human happiness due to the ignorance, prejudices and inferiority complex of his compatriots. In this sketch, he uses a candid story-book technique which contrasts sharply with the bitterness of the message conveyed. The episodes of the life of J.B. Laframboise are set into a frame story: on stage, a beautiful young girl, with long curls and a romantically beruffled dress, reads from a story book ''to all the little Canadians who are anxious not to waste their lives''—which sums up the theme of the sketch. The life of the hero of the story is told through a sequence of scenes, some only narrated, others acted out, but each one set against a painted background which gives the setting in the simple, broad lines of story-book illustrations for small children. In this way, we follow the progress of little Jean Baptiste from his birth in a quiet little French-Canadian village, through his early childhood and school years to adulthood. From the beginning, the complex personality of the child contrasts sharply with the candid simplicity of the pictures. When he is only four, his poor mother worries about his precocious intelligence: ''Ah, it's no good for children to be too bright: they start to sin earlier''. At school, he baffles his teachers by his quick and eager intellect. Eventually, the problem is solved to everyone's satisfaction: the dangerously clever little Jean Baptiste will become a priest. However, at the big collège, his omnivorous reading habits bring about his downfall. When he is finally discovered with a copy of Beaudelaire's *Fleurs du Mal*, his superiors decide it is time to step in. They summon his mother and inform her that her son is an unfit subject for the priesthood. The poor woman does not understand the meaning of the accusations levelled against her son ("Les fleurs du mal . . . is it some sort of poison ivy?"), but she does realize the full extent of the disgrace he has brought upon the family ("That's quite a disappointment, because it's a sure thing that the mother of a priest always goes straight to heaven . . . "). Jean Baptiste returns to his native village, his mind set on being a poet — a decision which turns not only his parents and all the villagers against him, but even causes him annoyance from the village dogs, "as it is well known that dogs always bark at beggars." The young man's serious internal conflicts are resolved once and for all by the well-meaning parish priest against whose arguments there is no further recourse, since he is presumed to have full knowledge of the will of God: " . . . you must remember that on this earth the parents represent the divine authority. Furthermore, if it had really been your vocation to be a writer, God would undoubtedly have enlightened your parents . . . . " Crushed under the authority of his ignorant and prejudiced parents, and the weight of his equally ignorant and prejudiced spiritual father's arguments, Jean Baptiste gives up his dreams and settles down to the respectable life of a village notary. Thereafter his life becomes an unending sequence of dull duties meticulously carried out. He accepts an ugly old woman for a wife, works hard to please his family, grows old in honor, eventually dies a peaceful death and appears before the Almighty. At this point, the tone of the work suddenly switches from satirical to serious, as the author points out the enormous waste which has taken place in the life of this man. Jean Baptiste is made to see the magnificent poems he had within himself all along, but which he never wrote, and he is crushed by the realization of his wasted life. He then addresses an impassioned plea to God to help his people achieve a better understanding of their situation and abilities to prevent similar tragedies in the future.

"I was nearly a genius . . . without knowing it . . . I never thought that could happen to a Canadian.

You see, God, the big failing of my people is that they have no confidence in themselves. They can't conceive the idea that a fellow who happens to be born in St. Agapit can be just as intelligent as another who happens to be born in Paris, London or New York.

It isn't very flattering to you . . . Because after all, God, being infinitely just, you couldn't do otherwise than give us as much talent as others . . . Only they don't understand that . . . It's funny, because as far as everything else is concerned, they are very Catholic.

And when a poor devil is born among them who has something on the brain, they won't admire him until he has gone abroad and been told there that he is a great man . . . So that's the only trouble, God."

While the satirical numbers of the Fridolin revues clearly served the cause of Canadian nationalism, the domestic tableaux provided light entertainment with a definite popular and québecois twist. In these realistic scenes from daily life, Gélinas realized his goal of providing his public with a mirror image of themselves which would make them laugh, and perhaps, having laughed, reflect. Broad humor, often bordering on farce, is the most obvious feature of these sketches, and the buoyancy of the performance invariably guaranteed that a light tone would prevail. On reading the texts, however, one is struck with the deep pessimism which underlies these comic sketches. The basic situations on which Gélinas builds his comic effects are situations of hopelessness and frustration, caused by a combination of factors: poverty, ignorance, prejudice, blind submission to clerical authority — the full spectrum of sociological problems which have traditionally plagued French-Canadian society. Gélinas has been accused of reproducing the conditions of life of his people with photographic realism, but this is not quite true. In these sketches, just as in the later plays which employ the same technique, he does practise photographic realism, but it is photography with a filter. The naturalistic setting is there, but the starkness is softened, the hard edges blurred as Gélinas skilfully develops all the humorous and farcical elements inherent in these scenes. In the revue numbers, the light-hearted element obviously prevails (although a reading of the texts makes one immediately aware of their basically pessimistic tone); in *Tit-Coq* and especially *Bousille*, the same naturalistic setting is still relieved by occasional touches of humor, but the plot lines clearly indicate the essentially tragic nature of the situation.

Gélinas uses two types of milieu in these domestic tableaux, the village and the urban working-class district. Scenes from rural life were not new in French-Canada, which, in the thirties, had gone through a great vogue of peasant literature with the *terroir* novels and poetry, but themes of urban life do not appear, even in the novel, which is traditionally more progressive than drama, until Gabrielle Roy's *Bonheur d'Occasion* in 1945. In introducing the life of the workingman of the inner city as early as 1937, Gélinas was as much of a pioneer in Canada as Zola had been before him in France.

The sketches are based on a number of stock characters which reappear, often with unchanged names, throughout the Fridolin shows. The same set of characters make up the cast list for *Tit-Coq*; in *Bousille and the Just*, the sociological background remains the same, but the characters have become more individualized and more clearly defined to fit the demands of the plot. *Yesterday the Children Were Dancing* is set on a different social level altogether, and bears no resemblance to the stock characters and situation of the Fridolin sketches.

The basic family group on which the Fridolin episodes are based is made up of a father, mother, assorted and varying younger people, and a maiden aunt. Father, mother and maiden aunt remain practically unchanged throughout the scenes and are taken over, prefabricated, to constitute the Désilets family in *Tit-Coq*. The father is invariably represented as a good-hearted and kind man who is bossed about by his wife and children; a man who has resigned himself to the very limited life-style which is his fate, and who seeks occasional solace in a bottle of whiskey. Obviously, this type of stock character lends itself to humorous treatment, and there are many good laughs at the father's expense throughout the sketches. If, however, we take time to analyse this father figure more closely, it becomes immediately apparent that we have here a recurrent pattern of frustration and impotence from which certain sociological conclusions could no doubt be drawn. It is interesting to note that this stock father figure in the work of Gélinas corresponds to the pattern of the father figures which emerge from the more avant-garde works produced by young French-Canadian dramatists in the late sixties and into the present decade.

The mother is usually sketched only in very broad outline: a hard working, no-nonsense sort of a woman, whose greatest claim to fame is the fact that she is a good cook. The maiden aunt, on the other hand, is drawn in detail. A character in which the ridiculous and the pathetic are inextricably mixed, this type would have an obvious appeal for Gélinas. Tante Clara, or Léontine, as she is also called, is the typical ageing spinster, butting into everybody else's affairs to cover up the emptiness of her own life. Loquaciousness is her main characteristic. Both in the sketches and in *Tit-Coq*, Aunt Clara is given long and exceedingly effective monologues. Her spinsterhood, of course, provides a great deal of scope for broad humor, but also for pathos, for Aunt Clara is a desperately lonely human being. Her attitude towards men and sex varies with the sketches: in some, she is comically appalled at the very thought of physical contact with the hated opposite sex; in others she shows an equally comic yearning for the pleasures she has never known.

These characters are placed in various settings: everyday life, special holidays, family celebrations. The general feeling which emanates from the texts is one of hopelessness: Gélinas has created here a set of characters who, we feel, simply cannot win. They are doomed by the circumstances of their life, by economic limitations, by lack of education, and even more by their own inner limitations: their inability to understand or to communicate with each other. Yet, on stage, each one of the scenes is highly amusing; some episodes are riotously funny. There, of course, lay the secret of the great success of the shows: the public could recognize themselves in these sketches, identify with all the miseries and hardships of daily life which they saw on stage, and at the same time experience the full relief of laughing at these same situations: a total catharsis. Gelinas' greatest achievement is not the social criticism inherent in his satires, for which he has received so much praise; he is not a reformer. Rather, his genius lies in his ability to redeem through laughter an essentially hopeless situation: although he describes all the horrors of living with merciless naturalism, he leaves his audience chuckling to themselves, and not at all unwilling to carry on, regardless.

As in the Fridolin sketches proper, the discrepancy between the ideal and the real is the recurring theme of the domestic tableaux. This discrepancy becomes especially apparent in the scenes which deal with conjugal life. It causes frustration which in turn is used by Gélinas as the basis for much comedy. The technique is particularly well illustrated in two connected sketches, "Le mariage d'Aurore", "Aurore's Wedding", and "Et ils furent heureux", "And They Lived Happily Ever After".

"Aurore's Wedding" depicts the preparations for the daughter's wedding day in an average workingman's home, with the usual array of stock family characters present. The author piles up one humorous incident upon another as a series of domestic mishaps occur, threatening the success of the big affair—minor tragedies which range all the way from the butter supply's running out to the drycleaner's delivering a wrong suit: predictably, it is the father's suit, and he is the one who will have to attend the wedding improperly attired. Adding to the general commotion is the presence of the maiden aunt, Léontine, who gives at regular intervals sententious statements about the folly of marriage, and every now and then, loudly thanks the Lord for having preserved her from the fate which is about to descend upon her poor niece. In an almost cruel way, Gélinas points out how all the higher and nobler feelings one associates with a wedding day are lost in the wild scramble to get the chores done. Everyone is cranky, irritable, and snapping at everyone else. The father maintains a modicum of philosophical calm, due to frequent trips to the whiskey bottle. The climax of the sketch occurs when the doorbell rings, and the bridegroom makes his appearance. Aurore, the bride, rushes to the door, expecting the delivery of another wedding present, but returns disappointed: "Ah, c'est rien que Theodore" ("Oh, it's only Theodore"). Obviously, the groom on his wedding day does not compete, in the eyes of his bride, with a butter dish or another set of facecloths! He rebels at this treatment, but we are given to understand that frustration must be accepted as a husband's normal lot, a lesson he has not yet learned but one with which the bride's father is quite familiar. In a spontaneous outburst of frankness, brought about no doubt by the combination of the excitement of the day and the liquor he has consumed, he confesses to Aurore that her mother, good woman and excellent cook though she may be, has never been much interested in love.

The same theme of the discrepancy between real and ideal is taken up in the sequel, ironically entitled "They Lived Happily Ever After". We find Aurore and Theodore a year later. It is evening. They are sitting in the shabby kitchen of a tenement building, Aurore folding diapers, Theodore holding the bottle for their three months old son. Both are obviously irritable, tired, and angry at each other. Meanwhile, in a superb take-off on the romantic illusions which surround the married state, the radio blares out a popular song in which the girl is asked to "be my spouse, oh divine one, and you shall know the ecstasies of unending nights of love . . . '' Aurore angrily switches off the set, and we soon discover the source of the marital discontent: she has been refusing her husband's advances, partly for fear of another pregnancy, partly because she feels that his lovemaking has become too routine and gives her no pleasure. Theodore, hearing this, walks out in a huff. Meanwhile, old aunt Clara comes to call, giving one of her inimitable monologues on the sorrows of the single life and enjoining Aurore to enjoy the blessings of the marital state while she can. When Theodore returns, he brings with him a peace offering of candy and peanuts and the earlier discussion is resumed. The dialogue runs on two parallel lines. One is an illustration of the human being's inability to communicate adequately his or her needs to another; it is a comment on the inherently tragic quality of the human condition. The other illustrates the battle of the sexes, with an overly aroused husband unsuccessfully wooing a recalcitrant wife; it is one of the archetypes of comedy, tried and tested since the *Lysistrata* of Aristophanes. Following the tradition, Gélinas makes us laugh at the expense of the husband, who eventually settles down for the night, unrelieved, on the living room sofa.

Similar broad farce, with an undertone of exasperation, is found in the two-part sketch ''Les parents s'ennuient le dimanche.'' This sketch is set in a workingman's flat in Montreal. Part one, Sunday morning, is a realistic portrayal of the first hour or so of family life after the alarm goes off on Sunday morning; part two zeroes in on the tribulations of the parents — again, mostly those of the father — during Sunday afternoon. Part one achieves its humorous effects mainly through familiarity: certainly, each member of the audience, at least those acquainted with family living, can identify with the morning rush: the fight over access to the bathroom, the last-minute tragedies in the way of missing buttons and lost socks. The mother stands steadfastly in the eye of the hurricane, while her young prepare to leave the house. Again, much of the laughter comes at the expense of the poor father, who emerges from the bathroom in his nightshirt, is immediately put to work, and eventually loses one item of apparel after another to the various emergencies which arise.

The second tableau, Sunday afternoon, presents life in a more quiet vein. Dinner is over, and the father, seated at the table, begins to cast amorous glances at his wife as she goes about her chores. Much craftiness and skill is expended in getting the youngest daughter, intent on finishing her homework, out of the house. Eventually, the child condescends to go out skating: the field is free. At this point, Gélinas inserts a series of highly entertaining manoeuvers on the part of the old man, who is obviously too much in awe of his wife to simply tell her what he wants. She does not seem unkindly disposed, however, and after a while follows her husband into the bedroom. Now, of course, follows the not unexpected ''surprise effect''; the doorbell rings, a friendly couple has dropped by, thinking that the parents must be bored all by themselves on Sunday afternoon. As the father, foiled again, appears in the bedroom door, cursing under his breath, the comic effect is assured, and he is greeted by thunderous laughter from the audience.

The realism, character development and style of dialogue in these sketches prepared the way for Gélinas' full-length plays. The last of the series of revues, ''Fridolinons '46,'' contains the sketch which was to be expanded into *Tit-Coq* in 1948. Gélinas abandoned the revue after he turned to writing serious drama; there was only one revival of ''Fridolinons'' in 1956, and it received mixed notices. The fact of the matter was that Gélinas felt that Fridolin had outlived his usefulness; he was no longer necessary. Comments on the contemporary scene could by now be made more effectively through film and by the chansonniers. Gélinas himself decided to serve the cause of Canadian theatre through playwriting and by providing an outlet for Canadian drama with the theatre he founded in 1958, the Comédie Canadienne. However, the importance of the Fridolin shows, and their impact on the French-Canadian cultural scene, can hardly be overestimated. In dramatic literature, Fridolin lives on through the characters in *Tit-Coq* and *Bousille and the Just*.

Notes to Chapter Three

1. Based on unpublished material made available to the author by Gratien Gélinas. All translations by the author, with the exception of *The Edifying Life of Jean Baptiste Laframboise*, of which there exists an English manuscript.

2. Maurice Duplessis, controversial Premier of Quebec from 1936 to 1939 and again from 1944 to 1959.

3. Cf. especially the plays published in *Théâtre Québec*, 1969 ff.

4

A Soldier's Return: Tit-Coq

"From tomorrow on, literary historians will no longer be able to say that dramatic literature does not exist in French Canada,"[1] wrote Edouard Laurent under the impact of the first performance of *Tit-Coq*. His feeling was shared by French and English critics alike, who felt that the play had effectively put an end to an intolerable situation. With the increased theatrical activity of the Forties in Montreal (the Compagnons, l'Equipe, the Théâtre du Rideau Vert), the absence of original plays had become more apparent, and more embarrassing, than before. True, there had been a number of attempts before *Tit-Coq*: in 1946, Carl Dubuc produced and directed his "féerie", *La fille du soleil* (*The Daughter of the Sun*), at the *Gesù* theatre; in 1947, the Compagnons had put on Felix Leclerc's *Maluron*; and Pierre Dagenais wrote a play, *Le temps de vivre* (*Time To Live*), which he produced with his own company, l'Equipe, in 1948. But none of these plays were of any particular interest, and they failed to make an impact on their audiences. Meanwhile, critics were keeping an expectant eye on the author of the eminently successful Fridolin revues, and multiplying their hopes, both verbally and in print, that Gélinas might succeed in applying his Fridolin formula to a full-length play. He responded to everyone's complete satisfaction. Nor was the enthusiasm generated by *Tit-Coq* a purely momentary phenomenon. While certain serious reservations have since been made as to the artistic merit of the play, its historical significance remains uncontested. Pierre Desrosiers' 1967 description of the central theatrical event of 1948 reflects quite accurately the general attitude of contemporary French-Canadian literary criticism about *Tit-Coq*: "While companies were being born, while producers and directors were slowly creating a (theatrical) awareness and building up a public, French-Canadian dramaturgy emerged from the void. As a matter of fact, it emerged with explosive force, with *Tit-Coq*, its first significant work . . . . "[2]

What prompted Gélinas to move from the revue, in which he was well established, to the difficulties and risks of a full-length play? In his customary tongue-in-cheek manner, he has provided us with an eminently simple answer to that question. It seems that one day, one of his sons, then eight years old, asked his father at the dinner table for a definition of the word "thaumaturge", which he had come across that day; and it turned out that in the child's mind, "thaumaturge" had come to be identified with "dramaturge" ("dramatist"). Gélinas senior successfully cleared up the misunderstanding, but the incident left him uneasy, and he decided soon afterwards that he would try to prove both to his son and to the world at large, that indeed thaumaturge and dramaturge were not interchangeable terms, as no miracle was needed in order to write a play. The result was *Tit-Coq*.[3]

Much more serious forces, of course, were at work in the genesis of the play. By 1946, Gélinas had perfected his dramatic skill beyond the needs of the cabaret style. As we have said, many of the Fridolin sketches were actually independent mini-plays, so that a full-length work seemed the logical next step. Gélinas was aware of the fact that such a work was now expected of him, and he had just the material for it. He had already dealt with the theme of the conscript twice in the revue. At the beginning of the war, his sketch "Le départ du conscrit" had been a natural in a topical revue, with conscription a highly controversial and emotion-laden subject in Quebec. When the war ended, his public demanded that he should bring his conscript back. Reluctant at first, he eventually complied, and the result was "Le retour du conscrit", in which he exploited the not very original situation of the soldier back from the wars who finds his girl married. Soon afterwards, he started to work on a film script based on the conscript theme, but gave up the idea of the film when he realized that he actually had in hand the makings of a serious drama.

He understood very well, of course, that "The Conscript's Return", while fully effective as a number in a revue, lacked the essential elements needed for a full-fledged play: a cast of characters, effective dialogue, characterization in depth, psychological conflict. It is fascinating to observe how these elements were worked into the existing framework of the original sketch.

"The Conscript's Return", like all the Fridolin sketches, was essentially designed to provide a vehicle for Gélinas' own talents as a monologist. It is therefore based almost exclusively on monologue. Even the confrontation scene between the returned soldier and the girl who has meanwhile married another has just enough lines for the girl, Marie-Ange, to lead into the soldier's speeches. In true cabaret style, we simply find the star of the show, Gélinas/Fridolin, this time in the role of the conscript, carrying on a long and informal one-way conversation with the audience, in which he tells them of his problems and misfortunes. For the play, it was clear that this format had to be changed to the traditional dramatic structure of acts and scenes (although traces of the revue style remain quite apparent in the structure of *Tit-Coq*, as we shall see later).

The character of *Tit-Coq* is modelled very closely on that of the conscript in the original sketch; but there is a radical change in the character of the girl, which makes for a totally different relationship between the two. The conscript already shows all the basic characteristics of Tit-Coq: he has the same easy-going nature, the cockiness which accounts for the title of the play, a way with the girls. Like Tit-Coq, this soldier is an illegitimate child, who has grown up in an orphanage, never knew his parents, and, like everyone else, would dearly love to acquire a family of his own. But because there is no serious conflict in the Fridolin sketch, his personality remains one-dimensional. The main interest of "The Conscript's Return" lies in the soldier's life generally; it is not focussed on his love story, as in *Tit-Coq*. He chats about his departure for the war, his time overseas, more or less casually brings in the disappointment over his girl's faithlessness, and ends up in a long monologue which goes off into social criticism — the difficulties of the returning soldier in re-adjusting to civilian life, especially at a time of economic recession (1946). In the play, on the other hand, there is a clear focus on the love story, made possible by a drastic change in the conception of the girl, Marie-Ange.

In the revue, Marie-Ange is just another eighteen-year old with a pretty face and a good figure who lets her soldier friend stay with her "every Saturday night until 3 a.m."; it is made quite clear that their relationship is based on mutual physical attraction, enhanced by the young man's special skill in matters of love. When Marie-Ange marries someone else, who can provide the security she needs, she misses her former boyfriend's caresses, but basically she is happy in her marriage. As for the soldier, he is quite willing to accept her decision, his main grievance being simply the fact that she did not write to let him know. However, as he concludes philosophically, there are many more women in the world . . . and he passes on to more serious problems.

The play is a quite different matter. Gélinas has constructed out of this raw material a gripping love story fraught with conflict. Marie-Ange here is the embodiment of all that is innocent, good, and pure. The love between the two young people is an idealized love, not to be consummated until after the war, when circumstances will again make a normal family life possible. To Tit-Coq, Marie-Ange represents the magic key to the happiness he has never known, that of being a member of a close-knit and loving family. When this Marie-Ange is pressured into marrying another, she finds only misery and unhappiness, and, regardless of consequences, she is ready to follow Tit-Coq, who returns to claim her. In this way, Gélinas has built up a situation of intense dramatic conflict, full of moral and social implications. The bastard theme gives the play a genuinely tragic dimension: the fact of his illegitimate birth lies like a curse over the life of Tit-Coq and determines his fate with tragic inevitability. Yet, the play is not a genuine tragedy. There is too much of Fridolin's humor, exuberance and indomitable spirit of "survivance" in Tit-Coq to classify him as a tragic hero; and, as well, the open ending of the play allows for the possibility of a positive solution.

Like "The Conscript's Return", *Tit-Coq* tells the story of a young man whose boisterous behavior has earned him the nickname "Tit-Coq" (literally, "Little Rooster"; "Cocky" would probably be an adequate translation). This cockiness on the part of Tit-Coq, we soon find out, is nothing but a defence reaction. Alone and unloved all his life, he feels he must constantly prove to the world that he can look after himself. An illegitimate child, born of unknown parents, Tit-Coq grew up in an orphanage, from which he escaped at the age of fifteen. A series of odd jobs eventually lead him to enlist in the army. When the play opens, we find him standing before his commanding officer, accused of having beaten up his best friend, Jean-Paul, in a barroom brawl. It turns out that the young man's wrath was aroused by Jean-Paul's having called him "a damn bastard", in total ignorance of the fact that the term, in Tit-Coq's case, constitutes not only the customary — and forgivable — insult among buddies, but also a very personal injury. When the truth comes out, Jean-Paul is ready to make amends. He invites Tit-Coq to spend the Christmas holidays with him at his parents' house in the village of Saint-Anicet near Montreal. The experience leaves Tit-Coq in a state of genuine culture shock. For the first time in his life, he witnesses the warmth, gaiety and love of a family Christmas. Gélinas has done everything to make the impact of the experience on a man like Tit-Coq fully convincing. Christmas in the Désilets' home is idealized and romanticised to the very limits of the acceptable: simple working class people, every one of them with a heart of gold, mellowed even further by the combined effect of family reunion, Christmas holiday and the occasional glass of whiskey, mother and father, brothers and sisters, uncles, aunts and cousins together give Tit-Coq a demonstration of family togetherness which makes him acutely and painfully aware of the emotional privations of his past life. The Désilets' home appears to him as a long-lost paradise, a paradise made even more glorious by the presence in it of Jean-Paul's lovely young sister, aptly named Marie-Ange. To Tit-Coq, who has grown up in rooming houses and cheap barrooms, and whose only contact with women so far has been the occasional streetwalker, Marie-Ange instantly becomes the embodiment of the Good, the True and the Beautiful. Marie-Ange returns his love, moved by the idea that, except for her, this young man is all alone in the world.

Their happiness does not last long, however, as Jean-Paul and Tit-Coq are soon transferred overseas. Tit-Coq takes with him, as his most prized possession, the family album given to him by Marie-Ange. As he paces the deck of the troop transport which is to take him to Europe, he lovingly leafs through its pages, rejoicing in his newly-found feeling of security and togetherness with "his" family. His favorite page, however, is a blank one, on which he pictures himself with his wife-to-be and their child. He could have married Marie-Ange before leaving, but, as he explains to the Padre, his steady friend and confidant, he could not face the idea of a child of his being born without his presence at the bedside. Because he himself has grown up without parents and without love, he wants his own child to feel the presence of both parents right from the start. And so, as he candidly confesses to the Padre, he left Marie-Ange, a "virgin and martyr".

Gélinas does not include in the play any details of the war itself. *Tit-Coq* was intended by the author as a psychological drama, and the historical events serve only as a background. While there is much local color in Act One, the second part focusses totally on the emotional impact of the protracted separation on the two lovers. Switching back and forth between Tit-Coq overseas and Marie-Ange at home, the author brings out fully the eroding effect of time on even the most genuine emotions. Marie-Ange has made a promise to Tit-Coq that she will not go out with any other man during his absence. But as the months go by, boredom and loneliness weaken her resolve. A former admirer, Léopold Vermette, pursues her incessantly. Instead of giving her some much-needed support, the members of her family, seeing her pining away, try to undermine her love for Tit-Coq and push her towards an alliance with the respectable and well-to-do Léopold. Eventually, unable to resist any longer, she agrees to let him escort her to a carnival ball.

Tit-Coq, at the same time, feels equally unhappy and frustrated at the impossibility of any genuine communication with Marie-Ange. Not only do letters take many weeks to go back and forth, but both of them have long since exhausted all of the phrases at their command to express their feelings for each other: there is nothing more to say, short of constant repetition. He becomes increasingly restless, anticipating the worst. Just as the war ends and he is about to be sent home, he finds his fears confirmed: Marie-Ange has indeed become the wife of Léopold Vermette.

In his first outburst of despair and rebellion, Tit-Coq reverts to his former ways of drunkenness and cheap women. But as soon as he returns home, he demands, and obtains, a confrontation with Marie-Ange. This final scene is a masterpiece of construction and dialectic. Having come only to accuse, Tit-Coq quickly forgives when he discovers that Marie-Ange still loves him and is acutely unhappy in her marriage with Léopold. He is now ready to take Marie-Ange away from her husband and start a new life with her, regardless of the fact that they can never be legally married. Marie-Ange, in a confusion of guilt, love, and shame, agrees to follow him. The Padre, however, intervenes. Recalling the past to Tit-Coq, he demonstrates quite clearly that what he has always wanted was not so much the physical presence of Marie-Ange, but the extended family with which she would have provided him as his wife, and from which they would both be ostracised under the circumstances. When both Tit-Coq and Marie-Ange realize that the illegal union they are about to enter would not only cut them off from any family ties but also reduce the child they might have to the very status from which Tit-Coq has tried to escape all his life, that of a bastard child, they see that the choice is no longer theirs. And Tit-Coq walks off, alone once more.

The major strength and appeal of the play is its dialogue. Through it the author has managed to create an environment and a set of characters which are fully alive and convincing. The structure of the work, however, lacks dramatic tension; it still points quite clearly to Gélinas' background as a cabaret artist, a weakness he was to overcome in his next play, *Bousille and the Just*. Tit-Coq is constructed along episodic lines, with thirteen individual scenes following each other much like the individual numbers of a revue. The action is spread out over eight different locations and takes place over a period of roughly three years. Because of this particular dramatic structure, the parallel with Brecht's epic theatre naturally suggests itself; but it should be pointed out that the ultimate form of the play was influenced more by Gélinas' general background, and the fact that it emerged from two cabaret numbers and a series of scenes in a film script, than by any Brechtian considerations.

In spite of its obvious failure to observe the classical rules of dramatic structure, *Tit-Coq* has been hailed by some critics as a masterpiece in the classical tradition. In Godin and Mailhot's, *Le théâtre québecois*, e.g., we find the surprising assertion that the play is constructed "according to the purest tradition",[4] with the exposition given in Act One, rising action and climax in Act Two, and dénouement in Act Three. While this is technically correct, the authors fail to observe the fact that the division into acts is purely one of convenience; the structure is determined solely through the sequence of scenes. The acts themselves are not nearly as cohesive as those in a classically constructed play, where each act forms an independent structural unit, composed of individual scenes which, although marked off from each other by entrances and exits, depend upon each other and their collective functioning within the act to fulfill their dramatic purpose. The individual scenes in *Tit-Coq*, on the other hand, represent complete small episodes almost as independent as the individual numbers of a revue, some of them not even essential to the development of the plot line (like aunt Clara's monologue). The looseness of construction is such, in fact, that scenes were shifted from one act to another by the author himself in preparing the English version, without such a shift affecting the internal organization in the least. Gélinas tried to achieve some dramatic tightening in the English version by reducing the number of acts from three to two, while leaving the number of scenes unchanged. The fact that the performance is broken only once, rather than twice, as in the French version, may contribute to giving the audience a somewhat more concentrated theatrical experience, but it does not affect the basic structure of the play. Instead of three acts with five, six and two scenes respectively, we simply have two acts with six scenes in one and seven in the other. Time and place are treated as freely in the English version as in the French.

But if the dramatic structure of the play is weak, the characterization, by contrast, is superb. Here Gélinas is in his own element. He had been experimenting with the creation of character since his early, school-boy efforts in monologue. With the domestic tableaux of the revues, he had perfected his technique, based mainly on his power of observation and his excellent ear for the nuances of the spoken language. Gélinas remains the first and, as yet, unsurpassed master in the art of creating a dramatic idiom for the French-Canadian stage. The secret of his characters lies in the superbly realistic, popular language which Gélinas has fashioned for them. Every line of the dialogue creates a living presence on stage.

The problem of a proper dramatic idiom has always been central to French-Canadian theatre. Its extent can be shown through the two extremes of criticism which have been directed at Gélinas. Conservatives and academics have accused him, in his search for linguistic realism, of "populism", of violating the purity of the French language in both syntax and vocabulary. Radicals, on the other hand, attack him for excessive restraint in not setting all of his dialogue in dialect (*joual*). The French-Canadian dramatist is caught between his allegiance to the cultural tradition upon which he builds, and whose language he must necessarily use, and his desire to reflect correctly the idiom of his own society. Paul Toupin's refined aestheticism[5] on the one hand, and the *joual* plays of Michel Tremblay[6] on the other, represent the two opposite, and equally unsatisfactory, poles in contemporary French-Canadian drama. Gélinas is probably the only one who succeeded in developing a fully realistic, popular language, respectful of the French-Canadian idiom, but retaining enough universality to make his plays understandable outside the *joual* community. Thus he was able to steer a middle way between the alienating effect of school French, and the overly limiting effect of pure dialect. He attributes his success in part to the influence of Robert Choquette, whose 1932 radio serial had already demonstrated that it was possible to re-create the language spoken by French Canadians without exclusive reliance on either classical French or *joual*. In an unpublished manuscript prepared for the CBC, he says: "I probably remembered this linguistic philosophy of Robert Choquette when, among the first in our theatre, I took up the challenge to express a genuinely French Canadian reality. I would have fought—and I did, in fact, fight—, for the right to use expressions which are typically our own. I remember that Jean-Marie Laurence, whom I consulted at the time of the publication of *Tit-Coq*, advised me strongly to delete the word "maudit" ("damned") and its compounds. But no! I found them indispensable . . . . (these expressions) seemed to me essential in the mouth of Tit-Coq, who had such a limited vocabulary to express strong emotions. But in all this, I constantly imposed upon myself the obligation to determine in conscience just how far I had the right to go too far, as the saying is . . . ."

Because of Gélinas' skill in handling language, even the supporting characters, though not fully drawn, come totally alive. An excellent example in point is tante Clara, Marie-Ange's maiden aunt (a character taken over unchanged from the revue). Her role is practically limited to one monologue (Act II, Scene

1). This scene has been attacked by some critics as irrelevant and superfluous; in fact, it is one of the most successful in the play. While not directly advancing the action, it is important in providing the psychological motivation for what is about to happen. In a play constructed along the epic lines of *Tit-Coq*, the insertion of such a scene is certainly fully justified.

Aunt Clara appears at Marie-Ange's on a Sunday afternoon, while the latter disconsolately tries to compose a letter to Tit-Coq; rocking back and forth with the irritating monotony symbolic of her life, the old woman goes into a long melancholy discussion of the dangers of waiting too long for a man who may never again appear, and the ensuing trials of the celibate life:

"... This blessed War! If only we knew how long it was going to last, we could plan accordingly. But no! ... And I do know what I'm talking about. If anybody can sympathize with you, my poor child, it's me all right. I might as well tell you, since everybody knows it, I, too, waited for one of those rare birds in the first war. When he came back, after four years and a half, he kept right on going, and settled on a farm in Alberta, the rascal! ... Mind you, I don't mean your own will do the same. He might very well come back, your Tit-Coq. From the little I know of him, he seems like a boy who could keep a promise. Even though such children, conceived directly in sin, I'd be surprised if they could turn out as dependable as others. Otherwise, there would be no justice for people conceived in duty like you and me ... but think about it twice. Because, if you only knew, my child, how quick it goes, our youth. So quick! You've got to be my age to realize it. You go to bed one night, fresh as a rose, suspecting nothing; next morning you wake up an old maid. And that's when you begin to rock yourself all alone Sunday nights on the front porch ... Yes, my child! There are times when it's far from being funny ... A good thing there's a God to make the portions equal in the other world...."

Even in the English, which comes nowhere near the zesty earthiness of the original French, the personality of the long-suffering maiden aunt comes out in full dimension. With just a hint here and there, Gélinas makes us aware of the emptiness of her life and the pathos of her religious philosophy, which clings so pitifully to a belief, at all costs, in that ultimate justice which would vindicate her in the end: the self-righteous reference to "people conceived in duty like you and me"; the relegation of all hopes to the next world: "a God to make the portions equal in the other world".

The author is equally successful with the other minor characters, even those which are barely sketched in. Like the traditional mother figures of "Fridolinons", Mama Désilets represents little more than a presence in the background. But Papa Désilets' good-humored remarks about her are enough to make her come alive. The old man has no illusions about his wife's intellectual capacities: "Mother Désilets, she didn't invent the telephone," (Act I, Sc. 2); on the other hand, his appreciation of her superb cooking comes through all along, together with some pointed comments on her embonpoint: "We can still feed you, you know, if we tighten up our belts a bit. For one thing, it will be good for your mother to eat a little less. And it will be cheaper than widening the doors to let her through." (Act II, Scene 3) Both parents are of course types, rather than fully drawn characters. But even as types, they are sufficiently individualized to escape the cardboard quality of the ordinary stock character. Old man Désilets may not show any particular originality in his idolizing of his youngest daughter, the pretty Marie-Ange. But when he refers to her as his "crée belle chouette" (an expression of endearment both rough and loving which the translators chose to leave in the English text unchanged), and teasingly threatens to make her sleep in the snow outside, *morsac*!, unless she has brought him a proper Christmas present, we cannot but experience him as a real person. These are characters conceived in the classic tradition of comedy.

The same is true, to a somewhat lesser extent, of the characters of Germaine, Marie-Ange's cousin and room-mate, and Rosie, the prostitute. The weakest character in the play is probably Jean-Paul Désilets, Tit-Coq's buddy and would-be brother-in-law. Because he serves exclusively as a foil to Tit-Coq, we tend to define him by negatives (unlike Tit-Coq, he is *not* quick-witted; *not* impetuous; *not* aggressive; *not* emotional in his reactions), so that his personality emerges as rather bland. Nevertheless, the character of Jean-Paul, undefined though it may be, adequately fulfills its function in the play.

While Gélinas insists that all of the characters are realistically conceived, one may question this assertion, especially in the case of the Padre, the down-to-earth, ever understanding and ever helpful army chaplain whom Tit-Coq seeks out as a father figure for comfort, help and advice. Like the Désilets family at Christmas, the Padre fully conforms to an ideal of perfection. While the total absence of any show of human weakness in the Padre makes him slightly unconvincing, this very quality does serve to make us accept the enormous influence he exerts on Tit-Coq in the final crisis. Had he not been able to build up in Tit-Coq total trust and confidence throughout the action of the play, we would hardly accept the latter's bowing to his arguments at the end.

Some serious questions might be raised about the character of Marie-Ange, which presents a grave inconsistency: idealized in the first part of the play, Marie-Ange is presented as clearly flawed by her weakness in the second. There is no possible doubt about the sincerity of her love for Tit-Coq in the early scenes of the play. She is an innocent and unsophisticated young girl. This is her first great love. And she abandons herself to it fully. The fact that Tit-Coq has no one in the entire world to love but her alone gives her an added sense of romantic fulfilment, and a sense of mission and responsibility. We are genuinely disappointed and somewhat surprised at the changes which take place in the second part of the play, changes which reveal Marie-Ange's great weakness, both physical and moral. We can follow Gélinas up to a point. It is not unconvincing that a lively young girl, who has cut herself off from all social life while her lover is away at war, should become restless, frustrated and melancholy as the months go by. It is not even unconvincing that she should accept the invitation to be taken out by a former beau, especially in view of the enormous pressure put on her by her family. But that Marie-Ange, Marie-Ange who has been presented to us as the Good, the Beautiful, the Pure, should let herself be pushed into a marriage with a man she does not love, while her feelings for Tit-Coq remain intact, — that move is pushing our dramatic credulity too far. The Marie-Ange of part two becomes a woman of such weakness that she effectively destroys the idealized image of the Marie-Ange of part one. Not only has she agreed to a loveless marriage, but also, when Tit-Coq returns, she is ready to follow him as though nothing had happened, showing the same thoughtless and selfish irresponsibility towards Léopold Vermette that she had previously shown to Tit-Coq. The character is, however, partially saved at the end of the play, when she is won over by the arguments of the Padre and encourages Tit-Coq to look elsewhere for the happiness she has not been able to give him. When asked about this inconsistency in the character of Marie-Ange, Gélinas replies that he fails to see that such an inconsistency exists. He explains the behavior of his heroine on the basis of the difficulties of the long, uncertain wait, the weakness of the flesh, and especially the influence of constant pressuring on the part of well-meaning members of the girl's family. The argument is only partly convincing. While there is no doubt about the depressing effect of a loving aunt like Clara on a restless and confused young mind, Marie-Ange's transition from ideal to ordinary remains an unsolved problem in the play.

The success of the work depends, of course, to a large extent on the title character of Tit-Coq himself. With Tit-Coq, Gélinas has extended the archetype which he had already created with Fridolin, and to which he added that dimension of universality which was needed to make of him a truly dramatic figure. Tit-Coq comes close to the classical definition of the tragic character, in that he elicits from the audience both pity and fear. But he is not a heroic character. Like Willy Loman's, his tragedy is the tragedy of the little man.

Enormous pity for Tit-Coq is aroused in the audience in the very first scene, when we are confronted with the fact of his illegitimate birth, and made to realize the warping effect which this illegitimacy has had on his life: "Christmas must be pretty exciting for you legitimates. It gives you a chance to hug and kiss from one end of the province to the other; but for guys like me, it's tame like hell. There we are, all alone on the street corner, since at Christmas even floozies join their families." For Tit-Coq, the awful prospect of spending the Christmas holidays in the lockup seems quite acceptable: " . . . I'd just as soon spend it in camp . . . . As I've got neither father, nor mother, nor uncles, nor aunts, nor cousins, that I know of, missing a family gathering won't send me sobbing on the floor.''

In a sense, Tit-Coq fits the Aristotelian description of the tragic hero; a good character, not entirely flawless, who suffers adversity through no fault of his own. While not a noble character in the traditional sense, Tit-Coq is certainly a good man, honest, sincere, and full of good will. His fall from the grace of Marie-Ange is brought about by forces totally out of his control: like the archetypal Oedipus, he is made to suffer for the accident of his birth. As in the case of Oedipus, the net closes upon him more tightly as he tries to work himself free: the very fact of bastardy from which he has been trying to escape from the beginning ironically reappears at the end, making it impossible for him to start a new and better life with Marie-Ange. The fate of Tit-Coq turns on two pivots, both tragic in their inevitability: his illegitimacy and the finality of the marriage contract for the society in which he lives.

In spite of these definitely tragic elements, Tit-Coq must not be viewed as a tragedy, nor is the central character a tragic hero. From a purely formal point of view, the play does not qualify as a tragedy because of its open endedness, which implies the possibility of a positive solution for Tit-Coq: it thus lacks the finality of conventional tragedy. Equally, it lacks that elevation of tone which we associate with classical tragedy: the raunchy, down-to-earth quality of the dialogue fails to convey a sense of tragedy, even though definite tragic elements are present in the play. Most important, the character of Tit-Coq does not come across as that of a tragic hero. Tit-Coq, hardened in adversity and trained to bounce back, no matter what, is too much the little man of the street, to make a convincing tragic figure. There is a pathetic air about him, just as there is about Fridolin. His fate may be tragic, but he fails to react to it in the manner of classical tragedy. There is too much pluck and joie de vivre in his personality for him to be labelled a tragic hero. His wonderful sense of humor, the cockiness to which he owes his nickname, his total irreverence in the face of authority all add up to a personality who may suffer reverses, but for whom final defeat is unthinkable. With Tit-Coq, Gélinas has created a fully realistic character, not an idealized hero. His reactions certainly lack tragic grandeur. When he finds out that he has lost Marie-Ange to another, he rushes out in a fit of despair—and we find him, in the next scene, blind drunk in a tavern. While the extent of his sorrow is made perfectly clear to the audience, his reaction cannot be compared to the high drama of Oedipus putting out his eyes, or Medea murdering her children in a grand gesture of revenge. Again as in the case of Fridolin, the author has successfully achieved his basic ambition, to create characters and situations as ''close to the people'', and as ''close to the reality of life in French Canada'', as possible. In the character of Tit-Coq, the public loved not only its idol, Gélinas, who was playing the part, but also the reflection of its own life with all its frustrations, its pathos and its tenacious desire for survival.

Not only could the public of *Tit-Coq* recognize itself in the characters of the play, they could also situate themselves immediately in the solidly realistic French-Canadian context described by Gélinas. The play certainly achieves the avowed aim of all French-Canadian literature, to remain close to the realities of life in Quebec, "coller à la réalité québecoise." Yet it was this very achievement which also earned Gélinas the disapprobation of certain critics, like Jean-Claude Germain and Michel Bélair,[7] who see in his objectively realistic approach a failure to awaken the critical sense of his audience. This is not a fair accusation, since *Tit-Coq* was never meant to be a play of social criticism, unlike Gélinas' later works, the bitterly satirical *Bousille and the Just*, and the political problem play, *Yesterday, the Children Were Dancing*. With *Tit-Coq*, the author simply intended to tell a story, and he has told it well indeed.

His approach here is undoubtedly less sophisticated than in the later plays. If there is a certain naïveté in his realism, there is also a great deal of charm. He accepts without question the three traditional central values of Quebec society, family, love, and religion, and shows how these values affect the lives of the people who cling to them. The Désilets clan represent an occasionally romanticised, but basically realistic version of the typical close-knit French-Canadian family. These simple country folk from the village of Saint-Anicet are drawn as close to nature as the wood sculptures of the Bourgault brothers. The fact that several members of the younger generation, like Marie-Ange, no longer live in the village, but have gone to seek employment in Montreal, correctly reflects the contemporary trend towards a gradual urbanization of Quebec. But even in the big city, the children retain their full loyalty towards, and affection for, the family. The importance of the family unit as the major motivating force in the life of the individual is brought out doubly in the play: in a positive way, by dint of the example of the Désilets family, and negatively, by showing the destructive effect which the lack of a family has had on Tit-Coq. The plot line itself underlines the same point. When Tit-Coq first falls in love, it is not so much because of the charm and beauty of Marie-Ange, as because of the warmth and security of the family group which she represents. When he goes off to war, it is not with a picture of his beloved in his wallet, but with an album full of the Désilets' family pictures under his arm. And when he finally resigns himself to a life without Marie-Ange, it is not because he no longer loves her, but because he believes that their love, cut off from all family bonds, can never be fully satisfactory. Love between two individuals needs the added social dimension of the family group to make it viable and meaningful. In all of this, the play accurately mirrors the contemporary climate of opinion of French Canada, just as the unquestioning acceptance of the finality of marriage reflects the social and moral context of the forties in Quebec. Divorce is simply not an operational concept here, as Germaine points out to Marie-Ange early in the play: "Yes, but remember, when you're married here, it's for a long time . . . . Getting a divorce is not easy in this province. We're a long way from Hollywood! . . . .

Down there, if you take the wrong train, it's simple, you get out at the next station. But here, you've got to go right through to the terminus.'' (Act I, Scene 5) At the end of the play, the decision of Marie-Ange and Tit-Coq to part forever hinges on this same social and religious problem, the impossibility of obtaining a divorce. American audiences found it difficult to grasp the full tragic inevitability of the young lovers' situation. In the French-Canadian context of the play, it is eminently clear: there simply is no other solution. It is this very element of finality which raises the play above the level of the melodrama, which it could easily have become had the action been set in a more permissive society.

As in the daily life of the province, the pervading influence of religion is felt throughout Tit-Coq. It is a largely unconscious presence, which subtly determines the characters' ways of thinking and behaving. In the play, Gélinas gives us the full spectrum of possible approaches to Catholicism, from the rather off-handed insouciance of Tit-Coq to the truly humanistic religious idealism of the Padre. There is a touch of caricature, too, with Aunt Clara, whose excessive religious zeal gives her the only possible outlet for her pent-up and frustrated emotional life. For most of the characters, though, religious observance is simply a normal and unquestioned part of the routine of living. Tit-Coq, however, whose sad life has given rise to a questioning bent of mind, looks at the demands of the Church with a certain scepticism. Even when he complies, it is for reasons of his own. Thus, he is quite prepared to treat Marie-Ange with all the respect due her innocence, but it is not because of any religious qualms: "Not for fear of sinning, or because we must not touch forbidden fruit. For me, that's all rather vague. Only, when you feel dirty, and you want to get clean, you don't foul the water before washing in it. Right?'' (Act I, Scene 3) Throughout the play, Tit-Coq feels that, since he has been singled out by his illegitimate birth, he cannot be expected to live according to the rules which govern the lives of those more fortunate than himself. He tries to make this clear to the Padre in their dramatic final confrontation: '' . . . Sin, you see, we were made in that, we bastards! Sin is our father, it's him who gave us birth; so we know him, and he does not impress us like the rest of Christendom . . . . God, I'll settle my accounts with him in due time. And I'm not worried. Because he has a broad mind, he knows good sense. If he's sneaked us into this world through the back door, he'll manage to get us into paradise the same way . . . ''

With the Padre, on the other hand, Gélinas has created a convincing portrait of everything a priest can, and should, be. He is a man whose deep religious conviction is never stated in words. Rather, it emerges through his genuine compassion and understanding for his men. In the very first scene, the commanding officer's affectionate reference to the Padre, "who, once again, minded my own business", shows the extent of the Padre's concern for his charges. He manages to win the full confidence of Tit-Coq by his patience and understanding, always ready to listen, even if the advice required is far removed from his ecclesiastical domain, such as when Tit-Coq wonders whether he should take Marie-Ange dancing or to a movie on their first date. He is liberal-minded enough not to bring in the commandments of the Church when Tit-Coq has sinned, or is about to sin, but always manages to bring him around to the right way of behaving by the sheer rationality of his arguments. He is always there when needed, but he also knows when it is time to drop out. In the final scene, he insists that Tit-Coq and Marie-Ange listen to his arguments: "You'll listen! Your own life's at stake in this moment, you've just shouted that yourself to Jean-Paul. I agree with you: it's worth talking about."; but he does not stay when the moment has come for them to make a decision: "Yes, I've said enough. (Deeply grieved) And I can do no more. Your lives are your own: you are free to spoil them, if you feel you must. (He goes out)". Gélinas himself insists that the figure of the Padre is not idealized, but realistically represents the average French-Canadian army chaplain; a statement which goes far to indicate the author's own high esteem of both the Catholic Church and her clergy.

Certainly, the play fulfills the three basic requirements of French-Canadian literature as stated by the literary historian Mgr. Camile Roy: French in inspiration, by its language; national, by its subject matter; and Catholic, by its religion. It is also the first serious French-Canadian play to fulfill these criteria.

To get a complete view of the impact and importance of *Tit-Coq*, we must look, not only at the play itself, but at its production history. As mentioned before, the French prèmiere of *Tit-Coq* took place on May 22, 1948, at the Monument National theatre in Montreal. Gélinas had spared no effort to make the production a success. He directed the play himself, in collaboration with his old friend, Fred Barry. No expense was spared in design (by Jaques Pelletier) and costuming (by Laure Cabane). The cast was headed by Gélinas himself, in the title role, assisted by a list of veterans from the Fridolin revues.[8] This assured him of superb ensemble playing, as well as an enthusiastic reception from an audience made up largely of Fridolin fans. The play, as we know, was acclaimed by critics and public alike and achieved a record run of over two hundred performances. Gélinas had given proof, with one master stroke, that Canadian theatre was not only possible, but even commercially viable![9]

Notes to Chapter Four

1. Laurent, Edouard, "Tit-Coq, un conscrit qui passera à l'histoire", *Culture*, Dec. 1948, p. 382.

2. Désrosiers, Pierre, "La nouvelle dramaturgie québecoise", *Culture Vivante*, V, 1967, pp. 71-77.

3. Anecdote told by Gélinas in his acceptance speech on receiving an honorary doctorate from the University of Montreal, January 31, 1949.

4. Godin, J. C., and Mailhot, L., *Le théâtre québecois*, Editions HMH, (Montreal, 1970), p. 35.

5. Cf. Paul Toupin's plays: *Brutus*; *Chacun son amour*; *Le mensonge* et al.

6. Cf. the plays of Michel Tremblay.

7. Cf. esp. Bélair, Michel, *Le renouveau du théâtre québecois*, (Dossiers Leméac, 1973), ch. 2.

8. Here is the cast list of the first performance:

Tit-Coq, Gratien Gélinas
Papa Désilets, Fred Barry
Jean-Paul, Clément Latour
Mama Désilets, Amanda Alarie
Aunt Clara, Juliette Béliveau
Marie-Ange, Olivette Thibault
Padre, Albert Duquesne
Germaine, Juliette Huot

To the above, all members of the *Fridolin* team, were added:

Commanding officer, George Alexander
Rosie, Mary Barclay

The first performance in English, on May 15, 1950, at the Gesù Theatre, Montreal, featured essentially the same cast, except for Robert Christie as Padre, Denise Pelletier as Germaine and Joy LeFleur as Rosie.

9. The English translation, by Kenneth Johnstone, is quite pale in contrast to the colorful idiom of the original. Obviously there are great difficulties in translating a work like *Tit-Coq*, whose popular idiom is deeply rooted in a particular cultural tradition. But it should be possible to come up with a more satisfactory translation than the present Johnstone-Gélinas version. Gelinas would be better served and his readers more rewarded with such a work.

5

Echoes of Ibsen:
Bousille and the Just

With *Bousille et les justes (Bousille and the Just)*, Gélinas established himself firmly as a serious dramatist. This play of scathing social criticism places its author in the tradition of Henrik Ibsen: like the problem plays of Ibsen's middle period, *Bousille* brutally reveals the faces behind the masks of social and moral respectability, and uses the concentration effect of the classical unities of time and place to increase its impact on the audience. It is the most gripping and most technically successful of Gelinas' plays; it is also the play which was longest in the making.

Gélinas had been preoccupied with the theme of *Bousille* ever since 1947, even before he finished writing *Tit-Coq*. But the work was not ready for performance until 1959. Gélinas is definitely not a prolific author. His record to date, three plays in almost twenty years, arouses the uneasy feeling that we are faced here with a man whose unquestionably great dramatic talent has gone largely unexploited. He himself partly agrees with this view; but he is also quick to point out that his life has been dedicated not only to playwriting, but to every aspect of the theatre — acting, directing, production and theatre management. When discussing these multiple interests, Gélinas alternates between pride in the versatility of his career and a feeling of regret at having been unable to concentrate fully on any one activity, and he eventually comes to the philosophic conclusion that, "*que voulez-vous*, one simply has to accept oneself as one is . . . "

The period between the première performances of *Tit-Coq* and that of *Bousille* is the most active and productive in the life of Gélinas. For several years, he was almost totally involved with the successful productions of *Tit-Coq*, in which he played the title role. At the same time, he was working on his next play. When television came to Montreal in 1952, he decided to try the new medium. On the pattern of the Fridolin show on radio, he created a weekly television comedy, "Les Quat' fers en l'air" ("Anything Goes") for the *1954* season, which he wrote and directed and in which he played the main part of Exubert Lajoie, a loquacious barber in an East Montreal neighborhood. Also during that period, he brought back for one last time the original Fridolin. Although the public loved the show as much as ever, the forty-seven-year old author decided that this must be his final farewell to Fridolin, as he could not very well go on playing an adolescent character (interestingly enough, the possibility that Fridolin might be played by another actor never entered his thoughts). The following summer season saw him at Stratford, playing Charles VI opposite Christopher Plummer's Henry V. And in 1958, he realized a project which had been on his mind for many years: the founding of the Comédie Canadienne, a theatre devoted to the production of original works by Canadian authors. When *Bousille* was finally ready to be performed, Gélinas proudly produced the play in his own theatre. For the first time in his career, the public identified him no longer with Fridolin, but saw him as the founder and director of Montreal's newest and most interesting theatre, a theatre which could compete with the well-established houses such as the Théâtre du Nouveau Monde and the Théâtre du Rideau Vert. In a press release issued in January 1957 Gélinas stated his purpose in founding the new theatre (a project which came about not without difficulty, and the success of which he termed "a small miracle"): " . . . to lay the foundations of a theatrical organization mainly dedicated to the production of plays by Canadian authors. Without ceasing to write for the stage, I intend in the future to put at the disposal of my colleagues in the world of the theatre the material organization which I have at hand and the experience I have acquired, to produce their plays . . . with the same care and devotion with which I would produce my own plays."[1] The production record of the theatre shows that Gélinas was able to carry out his aims: in the ten seasons of the Comédie Canadienne (1958-1969), thirty one out of thirty six productions were Canadian. Of all of these, Gélinas' own play *Bousille and the Just* was by far the most successful.

Bousille is essentially courtroom drama, but courtroom drama with a twist: all of the action takes place out of court, and the accused never appears. As in *Tit-Coq*, Gélinas' main concern is with psychological analysis, and the trial acts as a catalyst in bringing out the ugly realities in the character make-up of a seemingly respectable family group. Again as in *Tit-Coq*, Gélinas has chosen his characters from the lower middle class setting of his own native village, Saint-Tite; but they are not romanticised, as in *Tit-Coq*. Like Ibsen in *The Pillars of Society*, Gélinas reveals in this play the total depravity and lack of any moral or religious principles of his solid, churchgoing citizens, who will stop at neither perjury nor violence to gain their selfish ends.

The action of the play takes place within forty-eight hours in a cheap hotel room around the corner from the Palace of Justice in Montreal.

The play opens on the morning of the first day, as the Gravel family nervously settle in for their own private siege: twenty-four-year old Bruno, the youngest of the family, is about to be tried in a murder case, having caused the death of another young man in a barroom brawl. In a great show of family loyalty, all the adult members of the clan are present at this moment of crisis: Henri Gravel, the older brother of the accused and unquestioned authority of the family, with his new wife, the gentle Noella; Henri's sister Aurore with her husband, Phil, a good-natured cynic and tippler; the old mother, treated as an unavoidable nuisance by everyone; and finally a distant relative, simple-minded Bousille, who happens to be the key witness in the case. It soon becomes apparent, however, that, except for the mother who is intent only on saving her baby boy, the Gravel clan has come not out of any feeling of concern or love for Bruno, but only because they feel threatened by the situation — the family honor is at stake. The Gravels, as Aurore puts it, have always been "a respectable family", and the thought of being the target of disdain and malicious gossip in Saint-Tite is intolerable to them. "To think that for years we've moved heaven and earth so we could walk into church with our heads high — and now this big oaf gets us into this mess! ... It's quite simple: if he's convicted, we'll move and never set foot in Saint-Tite again." (Act I, Scene 2)

The lawyer, who comes in for a brief consultation with the family before the morning session in court, appears confident that he will be able to get an acquittal on the grounds that Bruno acted in legitimate self-defense, but the situation changes drastically after he interviews the two witnesses, Colette Richard and Bousille. Colette, a former girlfriend of the accused, reinforces the negative impression we already have of Bruno from earlier conversations: it turns out that Bruno (whose first communion picture ironically stands on the dresser all through the proceedings) has been nothing but a drunkard and a troublemaker all along. He had been tyrannizing Colette and beating her repeatedly for going out with Marc, a young man with whom she had fallen seriously in love. On Henri and Noella's wedding day Bruno had found Colette and Marc together. In a rage, Bruno attacked Marc, causing his death. The fight occurred in a small restaurant, and as the final blows were exchanged in the men's room, Bousille, who had followed Bruno to try to pacify him, was the only witness. To everyone's consternation, Bousille testifies that Bruno, not satisfied with knocking Marc unconscious onto the cement floor, hit out a second time at the prostrate man, shouting "this one is for your damned letter to Colette. And I've been saving it for you for two months." (Act I, Scene 2). This piece of evidence puts the case into the category of premeditated murder, with no further chance of acquittal. The simple-minded Bousille is totally unaware of what he has done and at a loss to explain the sudden hostility of the family towards him. As soon as the lawyer is gone, Henri, Aurore and even Phil decide that Bousille must be made to change his testimony, regardless of what measures may be needed to achieve this. Early the next morning, Henri sends the women away and with the help of Phil goes after Bousille. This scene (Act II, Scene 1) is a true masterpiece of development and dramatic tension, as Henri moves from pressure tactics, bribery and flattery to threats and finally physical violence of the most sadistic sort: by inflicting upon him intolerable physical pain, he finally succeeds in making the God-fearing Bousille swear, on the prayer book which Henri has forced under his hand, that he will not speak the truth in court. The dénouement follows with tragic inevitability: Bruno is indeed acquitted, but just while the family rejoices over the news, a telephone call informs them that Bousille has hanged himself and that they are wanted by the police for the inquest. In the true manner of tragedy, the net has closed in upon them, as they must face the very scandal which they have done everything to avoid.

It is an extremely powerful play, but a play which, unlike *Tit-Coq*, did not achieve its full dramatic force until after many changes and revisions. The play originally grew out of a personal experience. Sitting in a Montreal restaurant one evening during the Christmas season of 1947, Gélinas, always observant, noticed at the next table a family group whose gloomy countenance contrasted sharply with the general holiday mood; they were obviously country people who had come to town on some unpleasant business. The situation was enough to trigger the author's imagination: he imagined that the youngest member of the family might be in jail, and the rest had come to the city to attend the trial— hence their gloom. Realizing he had the stuff of a potential drama, Gélinas hastily took down some notes on paper napkins, which he filed away for the time being, as he was then working on *Tit-Coq*. Coming back to this material later, he realized that although he had the makings of a story, dramatic conflict was lacking. He eventually introduced into the story an outsider to the family, an old drunk who happened to hold the key to the testimony, and would therefore be brutalized by a brother of the accused. But he was not satisfied with the dramatic effectiveness of this new character: a worthless old tramp would hardly arouse in the audience the pity and fear at which the author was aiming. Finally, he conceived a different type of key witness: Bousille (*bousiller: to bungle*), a gentle, kind and faithful soul, somewhat simple-minded and deeply religious. Throughout the play, a parallel is drawn between Bousille, the family drudge, and Fido, the family dog: both lack physical attractiveness and intelligence, but make up for these deficiencies by their faithfulness and unending desire to serve. Inflicted on a victim of such childlike innocence, the brutality of Henri seems tragic indeed.

The character of the key witness was thus finalized, but the plot line was not. Gélinas wrote a first version of the play in which Bousille, following his perjury in court, goes on a drunken binge, and, returning to the hotel, dies of a heart attack. This ending, especially the long drawn-out death scene, attracted a good deal of unfavorable critical comment when the play was first performed in the summer of 1959. By the fall of the same year, the author had made some further changes, ending the play with Bousille's offstage suicide as it appears in the published version. With this new ending, Gélinas has made out of *Bousille and the Just* an almost perfect dramatic work. It is an essential improvement both from the point of view of the main character and from the point of view of dramatic structure. Bousille's death as a result of a drunken binge cheapened the character, and made him seem only marginally tragic. Having him kill himself as a result of unbearable feelings of guilt and total despair over his perjury, on the other hand, lifts him out of the ordinary, into the category of a truly tragic hero whose fate leaves us deeply moved. In the same way, the earlier long death scene tended to create an impression of melodrama and anticlimax especially following upon the tension-filled torture scene. In not actually showing the suicide, Gélinas followed the classical tradition, which does not allow violent events on the stage. Just as his use of the classical unities of time and space, this technique of restraint serves to heighten the impact of the event on the audience. It also helps to focus the attention of the public on the irony of the play's ending — ''the police want us back for an inquest''.

In structure, the play is more cohesive than *Tit-Coq*. The French version is based on a four-act structure, with three, seven, two and three scenes respectively, in each act. The large number of scenes does remind one of Gélinas' background as a revue artist. But in *Bousille*, these scenes do not break up the action into independent units, as they did in *Tit-Coq*. They are purely formal divisions unnoticeable to the audience. The author also specified that there should be only one intermission, at the end of the second act, so that the dramatic tension remains unbroken. The English version serves Gélinas' intentions even better than the French: here, the play falls into the natural division of two parallel acts divided into two scenes each, with each act corresponding to the events of one day. Act One covers the morning (expository scenes) and evening (testimony of the two witnesses, Colette and Bousille) of the first day; Act Two, the morning (torture scene) and evening (dénouement) of the second day. The English version has been further streamlined with the omission of some lines and the transposition of others.

Gélinas has been accused of indulging in his love of the picturesque in both dialogue and character and thus getting the play off to an excessively slow start. The real drama, according to some critics, does not begin until the appearance on stage of Colette, which would make the preceding scene dramatically indefensible. It is interesting to note in this context that criticism much to the same effect was levelled at Ibsen for the slow pace of the initial scenes in *Ghosts*! In the case of Gélinas as well as Ibsen, the slow and careful unfolding of character and background is of course essential, since neither writer proposes to present us with a suspense story, but rather with drama of intense social satire, and this requires a great deal of attention to detail. It is no doubt true that the action of the play could proceed just as well if Mother Gravel would not, at one point, waste much of her children's time and ours by refusing to sleep in the hotel without her beads, "like a floozie"; but we would miss the very essence of her personality.

It is through his masterfully drawn characters, rather than through the action, most of which takes place offstage, that the author develops the themes of his play. *Bousille and the Just* is a highly original dramatic work: with it, the playwright has achieved the difficult dramatic feat of running the full gamut from tragedy to burlesque without breaking the basic unity and coherence of the play. It is a richly textured work, which operates on at least four different levels simultaneously:

1. *Tragedy*: First and foremost, *Bousille and the Just* is a tragic play. In fact, it involves not just one, but two tragedies: the personal tragedy of Bousille, and the social and moral tragedy of the Gravels' behavior pattern.

2. *Social criticism*: *Bousille and the Just* represents a scathing indictment of the prevailing value system, whereby both religion and morality are distorted to serve the needs of surface respectability.

3. *Satire*: Supporting the social criticism of the play is a strong satirical underlay, at times going all the way into caricature, and directed at the exaggerations and distortions of religious devotion commonly practiced in the French-Canadian society which Gélinas presents with such merciless naturalism.

4. *Comedy*: going from verbal wit (Phil's asides) to situation comedy to occasional straight farce.

The four levels are meshed so skilfully that the work as a whole creates a fully unified effect. The secret of Gélinas' success lies in the creation of wholly believable characters whose interaction naturally results in the multi-level effect outlined above.

The tragic suicide of Bousille, based on self-condemnation and fear of divine retribution, is fully convincing because it has been carefully prepared all through the play. Scene Two of Act One, and of course the scene of Bousille's moral and physical destruction at the hands of Henri in Act Two, are particularly important in providing the necessary psychological motivation. The first scene (Act One) quickly outlines the character and his situation within the family: it is clear from the start that he is a man of unusual simplicity, whose kindness and naïveté are obviously being exploited by the relatives. But it is in the next scene (Act I, Scene 2) that we gain those essential insights into his character which make his later despair and suicide fully convincing. Through his conversations with Noella and then Phil, we discover that his life is governed by one ever-present, haunting fear: the fear that he might quite inadvertently do something to displease the Lord, and that the Almighty would then retaliate by letting him fall back into the vice of drunkenness, to which he once was addicted, as he candidly tells Noella, "for nearly seven months and two weeks", a period remembered with unspeakable horror. "Believe me, Noella, I'd rather be dead than fall back into that", becomes a statement of poignant dramatic irony from the perspective of the play's conclusion.

The scene with Noella has been designed to bring out the full pathos of this victim of his own credulity and innocence, who ironically blames his own weakness for the indignities inflicted upon him by his exploiters. Probing into the background of Bousille's addiction to alcohol, Noella discovers that it was all caused by the fact that mother Gravel, always worried about her youngest, had asked Bousille to accompany Bruno on his nightly jaunts to the tavern, to keep an eye on him and provide him with a sober chauffeur when he was ready to go home. Bousille complied for what he sincerely interprets as "a very selfish reason. When I'm not helping someone I get so bored." All went well during the summer, with Bousille waiting in the car until Bruno should have finished his revels; but as the weather became colder, he found it necessary to enter the tavern from time to time to warm his feet at the radiator. It was then that Bruno, already quite drunk by the time Bousille would appear, started forcing drinks on him. When it became apparent that Bousille was incapable of coping with the alcohol, Bruno found it a wonderful source of merriment to get him drunk and make him perform for the amusement of his drinking fellows. Within a month, Bousille, whose physical constitution is not robust, has become fully addicted to alcohol. There is an excellent and extremely revealing exchange of dialogue at this point in the French version which has unfortunately been left out of the English. Noella's reaction to the story is a sympathetic "Poor fellow!"; to which Bousille, with his customary selfless naïveté replies "Poor fellow, yes. I feel sorry for him, too: he should be more serious." His concern is still for Bruno, against whom he bears no grudge whatsoever! On the contrary, he feels almost grateful to the boy, who, "fortunately", as Bousille puts it, smashed the car in which they were driving one night against a tree, causing only minor injuries to himself, but landing Bousille in hospital for six weeks with a knee injury that was to remain painful for the rest of his life. Not only is it far from Bousille's mind that he could have sued Bruno's family for damages, thus achieving some small financial independence (he is now being paid a grand total of five dollars a week for looking after Phil's gas station around the clock), but he now calls the accident, "my lucky break." As he tells it, a certain Father Sébastien used to visit him in the hospital, and it was due to the magnetic influence of this priest that Bousille eventually managed to extricate himself from the living hell of his addiction. Although constantly tempted, Bousille now feels confident that he will always be able to overcome his vice, because, as Father Sébastien explained to him, "God, who is Almighty," will fight on his side, and "that demon of the bottle could never, never defeat both of us." However, the good father did not make God's cooperation unconditional, but instead impressed Bousille with the fact that he could count on his all-powerful ally only as long as he, too, did not fail Him by going against His commandments. Little did Father Sébastien suspect that this restriction would create in Bousille a condition of acute anxiety, an anxiety which eventually leads to his suicide. Because he depends so much on the good Lord to keep him on the path of sobriety, Bousille is terrified he might, even inadvertently, ''fail'' the Lord, which would automatically result in God's withdrawing His protection. In particular, Bousille is worried about the testimony he must give in court. Although he has gone over the events many times in his mind, and even laboriously written out what he must say, he is tortured by the idea of making a mistake: ''What if I forgot something, after swearing solemnly to tell the whole truth? That would really be failing God. His second commandment! — three before the one where he forbids us to kill! Then he would let me fall back into my vice for sure.'' This almost pathological fear of committing perjury is reinforced by a traumatic childhood memory which he recounts to Phil later in the scene. One of his uncles had caught his hand in a buzz saw just three days after committing an act of perjury — an obvious punishment from heaven which had remained forever linked in the mind of Bousille with that particular sin.

Following this detailed exposition of Bousille's state of mind and soul in the first act, the events of the second act take on a tragic inevitability. Phil and Henri's struggle for the soul of Bousille (Act I, Scene 2) is presented as a masterpiece of strategy and diplomatic manoeuvering obviously doomed to fail. The two men's clever efforts to camouflage the basic reality of their demand falter against the granite rock of Bousille's simple-minded, but correct understanding of the situation: what is asked of him is nothing less than perjury, and this he cannot and will not commit. Tension mounts as Henri, who tries to relax Bousille at first, increasingly loses his temper and gives vent more and more to the full brutality inherent in his nature, until the final, climactic act of sadistic cruelty. Phil goes along with Henri as long as the conversation remains amicable but retires in disgust when he realizes just how far Henri will go in forcing his will on Bousille. There is a great deal of highly effective dramatic irony at the beginning of the scene, as the two men appeal to Bousille's sense of loyalty to the Gravel family, enumerating all the supposed acts of kindness he has received at their hands—kindnesses which we know to be nothing but gross acts of exploitation. Bribery is tried next, and poor Bousille almost succumbs to the lure of a better job and enough cash to buy himself a motor scooter—until he realizes the price he will have to pay. When he again refuses to comply, Henri's patience is at an end. Brutally, he holds down the defenceless Bousille, kicks his injured knee until he almost faints with pain, forces some liquor into his mouth, and a prayer book under his outstretched hand, and eventually extricates from him the fatal ''yes'' to swear what Henri asks in court. Totally dazed, Bousille is led out of the room by Phil, and we do not see him again. When eventually a message arrives that he has hanged himself, this news

creates in the audience the classical reaction of tragedy: shock, pity and fear—
but certainly not surprise. The ending is fully convincing.

In a social and collective sense, the play could also be termed a tragedy, and
more particularly, a moral tragedy, the tragedy of a group of people not
intentionally evil, but whose perverted sense of values leads them to abandon
all moral principles to achieve their selfish aim. This social tragedy implies
severe social criticism, as Gélinas, like Ibsen before him, exposes the total
failure of the traditional value system (with its emphasis on family and religion)
to uphold such basic human values as truth and justice at a time of crisis. The
condemnation is both collective (the Gravel family as a whole) and individual,
with Henri and Aurore singled out as wilfully evil characters, and Phil equally
responsible through his weakness. The Gravel family presents the archetype of
the respectable small bourgeoisie, *du bon monde* who have never been in
trouble with the law, never absent from church on Sunday or from the sacra-
ments at Easter time, a family where the men drink within acceptable limits and
the women would suffer almost anything rather than give rise to doubts about
their virtue. Their entire life is geared towards maintaining, if not improving,
their social status in the community of Saint-Tite. Thus, they live by a code
which clearly allows private vices, but will not tolerate public ones. It never
occurs to them that their exploitation of Bousille might run contrary to the
Christian virtues they so ardently profess (charity is a concept they are not really
aware of); but when Bruno's trial threatens their reputation, they rise as one to
fight for the good name of the family. For Aurore and especially for Henri, it is a
fight with no holds barred.

As a counterpoint to Bousille, the character of Henri largely determines the
effectiveness of the play. For Bousille, Henri symbolically represents the cruel
and powerful ''Establishment'' at whose mercy he has been all his life, a tyrant
father-figure, as Bousille himself dimly recognises when he confesses that
Henri makes him think of his own brutal father. Henri himself has grown up in a
tradition of physical violence which he perpetuates, for inside his respectable
Christian home there also dwelt a father who took notice of his children only
when he felt the need to beat them. With the character of Henri, Gélinas has
illustrated brilliantly the tragic effect of the combination of this type of home
with the restrictive environment of a small country parish. Henri is incapable of
a single gentle emotion or noble feeling. The bulldozer he operates serves not
only as an outlet for his pent-up anger and frustration, but also as an effective
symbol of his way of dealing with the world at large: whatever stands in his way
will be broken mercilessly. The only element of the scenario not fully understandable with respect to Henri is his marriage to Noella, a young woman who
does not at all fit into the general picture of the Gravel clan: sincere, kind, and
loving, Noella seems totally out of place among her in-laws. To make the
couple convincing, it is necessary that the actor portraying the part of Henri
should combine extreme physical attractiveness with his violent character,

according to the author's stated intention: he should be "extremely seductive", *une belle brute* to whom the gentle Noella could conceivably be drawn by sheer animal magnetism and the attraction of opposites. Any interpretation of Henri as a physically, as well as morally, repulsive character cannot do justice to the play. Also, the contrast between the man's attractive physical appearance and his contemptible character further underlines the discrepancy between appearance and reality which is one of the basic themes of the play.

The critic Jean Béraud sees in *Bousille and the Just* "the most pitiless criticism ever" levelled against French-Canadian society.[2] This criticism comes across, not only in the unrelievedly naturalistic scenes such as the one between Henri and Bousille, but also through an element of satire which borders on caricature in the case of at least two characters, the old mother and Brother Théophile. The fact that Gélinas could openly present this kind of mordant satire of the less admirable aspects of French-Canadian religiosity reflects the social changes which had taken place in that society since the days of *Tit-Coq*, in which religion was treated with the utmost respect. By 1959, the general climate had changed immeasurably, due to increasing urbanization and most of all, to the advent of television. With the spread of television, French-Canadian society moved forward a generation in the span of a few years. The saying that television can open a window on the world proved eminently true in the case of French Canada, rural French Canada in particular. Television did away with the narrow parochialism which prevailed in all the Saint-Tites across the province and enabled French Canadians to achieve the necessary distance and objectivity for self-scrutiny and self-criticism. It was only natural that the Catholic Church, which had exercised such total authority over the lives of the people for such a long time, should be first to be hit by the new wave of liberalism and criticism of the past. Gélinas, always tuned in on every level to the life of the society of which he is a part, could not fail but to reproduce these new attitudes in his play.

The Gravel family illustrates all the various distortions of genuine Catholicism which had developed through the history of French-Canadian society. They use religion as a barometer of social standing and general respectability: "I'll swear she hasn't received holy communion for at least two years," says Aurore of Colette, indicating the utter worthlessness of the character. The women use it as a means of exercising authority over the men, forced, much to their exasperation, to take part in the pilgrimages and other religious devotions vowed by the women in moments of crisis. To the old lady, religion is a means to force her grown-up children into togetherness and submission: when she categorically announces that everyone will participate in the family rosary broadcast over the radio, no one, not even Henri himself, dares contradict. Most important, religion is seen as a means of obtaining from the powerful hierarchy of angels and saints which leads up to the Almighty all those things not easily available otherwise. In other words, religion for the Gravel clan and the society they represent is a social factor, a routine in living, and a potential source of benefits. It is definitely not a spiritual matter; not even a moral matter, as they are scarcely aware of the ethical dictates of Christianity. Bousille alone takes religion seriously in the sense of recognizing that his faith in God demands from him in turn a certain type of behavior, but even with Bousille, this adherence to the principles of morality, when it is not instinctive, is based on fear, not love, of the Lord. The only character who embodies genuinely Christian principles is Noella, whose function in the play is purely supporting.

With the characters of Brother Théophile and the mother, religious satire goes all the way into caricature. It is a tribute to the comic talent of Gilles Latulipe, who played the part of the little Brother in the première performance, that the audience burst out laughing simply when he appeared, not even waiting for his first line. This reaction also indicates the enormous need of the contemporary audience for the liberating effect of this type of satire.

The seventeen-year old Théophile, a pure in heart whose life has been spent in the novitiate since the age of eleven, is brought in by his proud half-brother Bousille to assist the old lady in the agonies of the long wait for the outcome of the trial. On the contrary, the confrontations leave mother Gravel in greater despair than ever, as Théophile in his innocence attempts to comfort her with the heroic example of martyrs through the ages, topping off his exhortations with the gift of a medal of St. Jude, patron saint of hopeless causes. The discrepancy between the self-centered religiosity of the old lady, and the idealism of Théophile runs throughout these dialogues. It can be summed up in one brief exchange:

Théophile: As for me, I'll pray that justice be done.
Mother: Pray that we win: that's all I ask!

With the second appearance of Théophile, the tone changes from amusing caricature to one of bitter irony. The trial is over, and as Théophile bids good-bye to the family, he candidly thanks them for everything they have done for his poor Bousille, until even the cynical Phil is barely able to bear the weight of the accusation unwittingly implied by the young innocent. The scene is an excellent example of Gélinas' ability to blend together successfully such diverse elements as caricature, satire and tragedy.

Mother Gravel provides another effective caricature of the ''good Catholic'': she carries a picture of Saint Anne in her purse, cannot spend a day without her beads, bribes heaven with all she thinks most effective in order to obtain the favor she wants, and manages to live blissfully oblivious to the most elementary dictates of genuine Christianity.

Besides caricature and satire, the tragedy of Bousille, as mentioned before, also contains some genuinely comic elements, which range from farce to verbal wit and double entendre. Gélinas has been criticized for incorporating into a serious play some undeniably coarse episodes: Phil's rush for the bathroom at the beginning of the play, mother Gravel's relieved appearance, again from the bathroom, carrying her bothersome corset in her hand. Certainly, these details are dramatically unnecessary and could be eliminated in the interest of good taste. But such a deletion would eliminate not only a few laughs, it would do away with the author's intention to give vivid illustrations of the obvious vulgarity of the Gravel family. The characters of this tragedy express themselves not in classical Alexandrines but in the colorful, if occasionally coarse, idiom of rural French Canada; by the same token, they cannot be held to the refined behavior patterns of the characters in a classical tragedy. Vulgarity is an essential part of their personality; in a naturalistically conceived work, representation of such vulgarity on stage should not be objectionable.

Even when presenting a tragedy, Gélinas never departs from his basic purpose, that of entertaining the audience. In *Bousille*, this result is achieved mainly through the unceasing flow of witticisms and cynical asides from Phil Vezeau. Phil's sense of humor is such that he emerges as a rather lovable character in spite of his drinking, philandering, and, above all, his weakness in going along with the wishes of Henri. Because he is clever and never fully serious (a possible result of the fact that he is never fully sober, either), we are amused by his antics when we should be shocked. He tells Bousille he has to make "a confidential call to the President of the Children of Mary", and, no sooner alone, fixes a rendezvous with a local prostitute. His clever remarks are totally lost on the rest of the family, creating an additional touch of delightful irony for the audience. Thus, his sarcastic reaction to Bruno's acquittal is completely missed by the members of the family, but does not fail to inject a note of bitterness into the otherwise jubilant atmosphere, such as when he counters his wife's remark that they must pick up a doll for their little girl on the way home with a muttered "And I'll try to find a nice little black-jack for Gaston: that child should be learning how to get along in the world."

Some painfully comic effects are achieved even through the character of Bousille himself, whose excessive naïveté leads him to misunderstandings and misinterpretations of all kinds. There is a humorous element also in the incongruity between Bousille's simple and limited manner of expressing himself on all worldly concerns, and his adoption of the stilted and grandiloquent formulations of the Church as soon as religious matters are involved: "que je suis donc faible devant la souffrance corporelle," he says as he is having his finger disinfected by Noella, a statement whose impact has been lost in the official English translation: "I am such a crybaby . . . "

Generally speaking, the translation (by Kenneth Johnstone and Joffre Miville-Dèchene) is superior to the translation of *Tit-Coq*, (by Kenneth Johnstone in collaboration with Gratien Gélinas) although it suffers from some of the same weaknesses. In structure, the English version, as was said earlier, represents a definite improvement over the French. In the process of streamlining and adaptation for an audience with a different cultural background, however, some very effective elements have inevitably been lost. Parts of the rosary episode in the first scene have been deleted in the English version, as well as brother Théophile's long exhortations on the example of Job (end of Act 1). As in *Tit-Coq*, the English dialogue as a whole seems somewhat anemic compared to the French, again for the same reasons. Gélinas' dialogue captures the spirit of his characters from Saint-Tite so realistically that a full transposition into another cultural background is simply not possible.

In spite of the weaknesses of translation, the play was well received in English, and enthusiastically in French. The première performance took place on August 17, 1959, at the Comédie Canadienne, under the auspices of the annual Festival de Montréal.[3] The première was followed by over three hundred performances in twenty-six Canadian cities. *Bousille* is definitely the best dramatic work produced by Gélinas to date, a work which is certain to remain an important part of the French-Canadian repertory.

Notes to Chapter Five

1. Gélinas, G., "Credo of the Comédie Canadienne", *Queen's Quarterly*, LXVI, Spring 1959.

2. Béraud, Jean, reviewing the play in *La Presse*, August 18, 1959.

3. The cast of the première performance was the following: Bousille, Gratien Gélinas; Henri, Yves Létourneau; Phil, Jean Duceppe; Aurore, Béatrice Picard; Noella, Nicole Filion; Mother, Juliette Huot; Colette, Monique Miller; Brother Théophile, Gilles Latulippe; Lawyer, Paul Hébert.

6

Fathers and Sons:

Yesterday the Children Were Dancing

The three major plays of Gratien Gélinas provide clearcut landmarks of the three major stages in the evolution of French-Canadian consciousness: *Tit-Coq*, 1948, reflects the uncritical acceptance of the status quo; *Bousille and the Just*, 1959, self-appraisal and self-criticism; and finally, *Yesterday the Children Were Dancing*, 1966, the realization of the need for change. Looking back upon the three plays, one can see a definite evolution in characterization and especially in structure, from the rather loosely connected scenes of *Tit-Coq* to the sophisticated structural pattern of the last play. In his treatment of the two major motive forces of French-Canadian society, religion and the family, change is also apparent. *Tit-Coq* idealizes the family and pays homage to religion through the character of the Padre. In *Bousille*, the myth of the loving family is destroyed, and conventional religiosity exposed through caricature. *Yesterday the Children Were Dancing* does not deal with the issue of religion at all, but does focus on the problem of the family. It represents Gélinas' most sophisticated approach, combining idealization with a profound pessimism. The two generations of the Gravel family provide an eloquent illustration of the fact that even under the most ideal circumstances, a family unit may not remain viable in the long run — not through anyone's fault but simply because of the human condition.

With this drama, as always, Gélinas remains faithful to his original formula, *coller à la réalité québecoise*, to remain close to the social and psychological facts of life of his milieu. The differences between this work and the earlier ones are therefore not dictated by any esthetic principles, but rather they arise organically out of the fact that essential changes had taken place in French Canada in the intervening years. As observers of the French-Canadian scene have pointed out, the years after the Second World War count double and triple in the evolution of that society; from the point of view of social, and economic development, and general awareness, an entire generation lies between each one of the works of Gélinas. It is an accurate reflection of the historical situation, therefore, that Tit-Coq should be a hero of acceptance and resignation, and André Gravel, a hero of revolution. Tit-Coq would have been a terrorist, in 1966.

The nationalism of French-Canadian youth in the early sixties should be understood as part of the general critical awakening which had begun during the war years. "After calling to task our relationship with the Church, our educational system, our economy, the same critics are turning today on our political structures . . . . Youth's sudden attack on Confederation is but the extension of their self-questioning over the past fifteen years", wrote Gérard Pelletier in 1961.[1] For a brief period, these attacks took on the form of a wave of terrorist violence — the background against which Gélinas sets his play.

The issues which ultimately led up to the events of 1963 were clear-cut and down-to-earth: Quebec, on the road to greater social and economic progress, demanded greater control over its fiscal system, and independence from joint federal-provincial programmes in the areas of education, public health and welfare; and it protested the unilateral application of the principle of bilingualism. Above and beyond these rational demands, however, was the full and complex emotional overlay which normally clouds the problems of minority groups. The impending centenary celebrations further contributed to the creation of a sense of urgency: Daniel Johnson, leader of the Union Nationale, had termed the years between 1963 and 1967 "the years of our last chance", a phrase which proved dangerously felicitous. The character of André Gravel, the terrorist hero of *Yesterday the Children Were Dancing*, becomes fully convincing in the light of the fiery rhetoric produced during these years, rhetoric which aroused in the pre-war generation a sense of déjà-vu, but which could not miss in its effect on the very young. A good example in point is Marcel Chaput's statement, *Why I am a Separatist*, which not only sets down the four basic principles of the movement ("The French Canadians form a nation; The French-Canadian nation is a nation like any other; Quebec is the rightful state of the French Canadians; To progress, French Canadians must be masters of their own home"), but goes on to the kind of demagoguery even well-read and intelligent adolescents find hard to resist: "I cannot stand by silently, as others seemingly can, and watch the day-by-day extermination of my people . . . . Separatism . . . independence, liberty, fulfilment of the nation, French dignity in the new World . . . ."[2] As a result of this and similar inflammatory rhetoric, a series of bombings took place in Montreal in 1963, killing one man and maiming another. When the terrorists were apprehended, the general reaction in French Canada was one of shocked surprise. As one woman expressed it in a letter to a daily paper, "it could have been my son!" — for the feared guerrillas turned out to be not foreign bandits, but young French Canadians from all walks of life. It is this particular psychological aspect of the situation that Gélinas chose as the theme for his play: the tragic, and traumatic, conflict between the generations at a time of crisis. *Yesterday the Children Were Dancing* is less a political play than a psychological drama on the universal theme of fathers and sons. The particular political events which occurred in Montreal in 1963 provided him with the perfect context in which to develop this theme; aside from this, they are of no further interest to Gélinas. ''I am not interested in politics, I am interested in telling a story'', he says in reference to the play. It is of course understandable that the political aspect of this drama should have been taken very seriously at the time, since it dealt with events which were, after all, highly topical. However, the abiding merit of the play certainly does not lie in its topical value (self-revealing though it might have been to both English and French Canadians at the time); it lies in its realistic and compassionate treatment of a universal theme.

The history of the play's title gives a good indication of how very closely this drama reflects the social, political and personal tensions of the period. Gélinas had been given a poem written in prison by a young man whose own political and family situation approximated that of André Gravel in the recently completed, and yet untitled, play. This prison poem contained the line ''les enfants dansaient hier'', a line which caught the imagination of Gélinas. He transposed the words to the more euphonic ''hier, les enfants dansaient'' and used them as a fitting title to his play. This effective phrase, rich in nostalgic connotations, is also built into the text of the play (Act II, Scene 8).

Yesterday the Children Were Dancing also reflects certain aspects of the author's personal life. At the time of composition, Gélinas, too, had sons in their early twenties, and although politics was not a burning issue in his family, he certainly had direct insight into the complexities of the conflict between the generations. In the Gélinas household as in the Gravel home, growing sons found themselves face to face with a highly respected and more than averagely successful father — a situation fraught with potential conflict. The upper-middle-class setting of the play, with its emphasis on comfort and elegance, brings it close to the author's own lifestyle: like the Gravels, the Gélinas family divided their time between a city home in Montreal and a Laurentian retreat. In the idealized character of Louise, the mother, Gélinas pays tribute to his first wife, and mother of his children, Simone Lalonde;[3] like Louise, a French Canadian with a touch of Irish. The closeness of the relationship between the Gravel couple reflects Gélinas' own idealistic view of marriage, just as the mutual love and respect between the two generations of Gravels represents the author's own ideal of the united family — an ideal which Gratien Gélinas, unlike Pierre Gravel, managed to carry over beyond the period of his children's adolescence.

The plot line of the drama is quite simple. The action is set in Montreal, at a moment when political tensions are running high because of an impending federal election. The Minister of Justice has died suddenly of a stroke, and

Pierre Gravel, an eminent lawyer, federalist and longtime worker for the Liberal party, has been asked to run in his riding, with the assurance that he will be given the cabinet post if elected. For Pierre Gravel, this post would mean the fulfilment of his lifelong ambition; however, he will not accept until he has consulted the members of his family. To his shock and surprise, it turns out that his older son André, whose separatist leanings were not unknown to Pierre, is actually the leader of the terrorist movement which is currently organizing a series of bombings across the province; André himself is due to set off a bomb and turn himself in to the police that very evening. Obviously, the father of a terrorist leader cannot aspire to the post of Minister of Justice in the Federal Government. There is no arguing with André's laconic "You have to refuse: you've no choice." (Act I, Scene 5) — unless André can be persuaded to give up his position.

The entire second act of the play is devoted to the confrontation between the generations, with André and his girl friend, Nicole, facing Pierre Gravel, the father, and Paul O'Brien, Pierre's brother-in-law and partner in his law firm. When Louise appears on the scene, the weight of the battle shifts from the theoretical to the emotional, as the mother's love goes out equally to her husband and her son. Eventually, the logic of the situation itself dictates its outcome: André goes off to do what he must, and Pierre, only partly defeated, returns to the speech he was composing earlier, in which he sets down the unchanged principles which govern his own political morality.

Unlike Gélinas' earlier plays, *Yesterday The Children Were Dancing* does not derive its main effectiveness from the picturesque nature of the characters, but rather from an extremely successful dramatic structure. As in the problem plays of Bernard Shaw, the characters stand mainly as representatives of certain ideas: the essence of the play lies in the confrontation of these ideas. Yet, Gélinas has not presented us with a theoretical treatise in dialogue form, on certain political and psychological issues. He has presented us with a gripping and totally human drama. He achieves this through the careful build-up of the action, the unobtrusive interweaving of the father and son plots, and the repeated surprise effects, in part one of the play; and through a superb organization of the arguments themselves into a number of rounds of verbal battle with increasing emotional impact in part two. The structure is not altogether flawless, of course. There are moments when the dramatic movement is retarded unnecessarily, such as the reading out of the entire terrorist manifesto (Act II, Scene 6), or the reading of André's letter to his mother (Act II, Scene 7); but by and large, Gélinas has managed to retain the elements of suspense and dramatic tension in a play which deals largely with theoretical issues. The fact that the author does not take sides, but presents the two parties with equal conviction, no doubt contributes to the impact of the play: in this way, it is the conflict itself, rather than a particular ideology, which becomes the subject matter. And conflict is, after all, the essence of drama—just as propaganda is its antinomy.

Yesterday the Children Were Dancing, like *Bousille and the Just*, makes full use of the concentration effect of the classical unities of time and space: the entire action takes place within a few hours, in the Gravels' living room. The play is formally divided into two acts, with a total of eight scenes, but the action continues unbroken, as Gélinas points out in the stage directions: "The action of the play unfolds without interruption. As a courtesy to the audience, however, the curtain falls at the end of Scene Five. When it rises again after Intermission, the characters are found in exactly the same situation in which we left them."

Although the action itself remains unbroken, the division of the play into two parts corresponds to an organic development: part one brings the action to the climactic moment of André's revelation, while part two explores the psychological conflicts which arise out of this revelation. The final scene brings both lines of the action to a logical conclusion, without resolving the psychological or the political conflicts.

The play builds slowly to the climax. Gélinas uses a dramatic technique which is extremely effective: starting out on a rather light note, he gradually turns an apparently unproblematic situation into inescapable tragedy. The first two scenes especially are treated more like the opening scenes of a comedy than those of a serious play. Gélinas excels in the creation of comic characters, and in this play he allowed himself the intrusion of such a character at least for the initial two scenes. Roberge, the Liberal party organizer who tries to high-pressure Pierre Gravel into accepting the nomination is a typical Gélinas character, cast in the mold of Fridolin. His speech has the same typically French-Canadian earthiness and robust humor, his single-mindedness of purpose in pushing Gravel towards his political goal is comically exaggerated, and his final exit is made into a veritable clown act. These first two scenes also give the two main plot lines: Gravel's nomination, which appears to be the main theme, and the fact of terrorist activities occurring in the province. The latter, however, are mentioned only in passing, so that the audience, following the lead of the characters, fails to attribute much importance to these incidents—to be all the more shocked when their significance is revealed later on in the play. A light, almost bantering tone is maintained throughout the first two scenes. With the disappearance of Roberge, however, the drama takes on a more serious tone. In scene three, Gravel and his brother-in-law discuss the issue quietly among themselves. This scene does little to advance the action, but it does fulfil an essential function in the play, by throwing light on every aspect of Pierre Gravel's public and private life, as he passes under review the members of his family and tries to anticipate their reactions. He has no fears about Louise, who is presented throughout as the epitome of the perfect wife, "an attractive girl with a strong enough personality to keep up with you on the road to success", (a feminine ideal perhaps not quite in keeping with the gospel of Women's Liberation, but fully in accordance with the views of Gélinas).

Having considered the wife, the two men now turn to the sons. Larry, the younger one, presents no obvious problem, as he is easygoing and just now seems intent only on playing his guitar. André, the older one, as Gravel realizes, presents a more serious difficulty: brilliant, headstrong and rebellious, he has already let his father know that he disapproves of his federalist convictions. However, Gravel feels confident he can persuade even André of the reasonableness of his decision. The scene is skilfully constructed to carry out a number of functions: it brings into the play the important information about André's separatist leanings; more significantly, it prepares the ground for the family tragedy by showing the full extent of the love of all the members of the family for each other, and, ironically, it portrays the father's special love for André, his favorite. The dialogue comes dangerously close to sentimentality when Pierre Gravel reminisces about the happy times he used to spend sailing on the lake with André when the boy was little, and the author insists on letting us know that even now, father and son form a perfect team: '' . . . when we go off alone, just him and me, on the lake in the sailboat. There, Paul, we're not two beings, we're one . . . . '' Finally, Gélinas foreshadows the pathos of the impending conflict in this early scene, by bringing in the speech Gravel is preparing for the Canadian Club of Toronto. He has given it a radical tone calculated to impress, not so much his audience, but the son whose good will he desires: "The first person I want to get it across to is André. He must understand that 'valiant defenders of our threatened country' can be found inside the fort as well as outside." His brother-in-law, Paul O'Brien listens approvingly, and agrees, with the naïveté and lack of comprehension of the older generation for the young, that "It might help him accept your candidacy".

André having thus been introduced — most favorably — through his father's comments, is shown once more from yet another indirect point of view in scene four. This scene introduces Nicole, a university student, pretty, charming, intelligent, and head over heels in love with André, whose determination and leadership she admires. André's picture now becomes somewhat more complex. To the older generation, he is simply a brilliant young law graduate who "hasn't found himself" yet and therefore is bound to act somewhat strangely at times. Nicole, however, realizes that there exists an extremely serious dimension in André's life to which she has no access. With great care not to offset the shock effect of André's revelation in the following scene, Gélinas builds up through the character of Nicole the data needed to make this revelation appear logical. Nicole knows that André loves her, but he has warned her not to think of marriage yet: '' . . . he told me last week I'd better get used to the idea of not seeing him for a few months . . . . Said he was going on a long trip . . . and when he came back maybe we could talk about serious things — if I went along with his reasons for going there.'' Nicole assumes nothing more frightening behind these cryptic remarks than some plan to work in an underdeveloped country, and the scene again steers clear of tragedy. On the contrary, Gélinas manages to include some light humorous relief through the confrontation of the two middle-aged gentlemen with the pretty and outspoken Nicole.

The spokesman for the generation of young radicals finally appears in the last scene of Act One. An extremely clever dramatic device adds to the impact of this long-awaited appearance. André makes his entrance just as his father is talking on the telephone to Lester B. Pearson, who has called from Ottawa to express his good wishes concerning his nomination. The situation is calculated to illustrate the juxtaposition of forces and their tragic interaction. Federalism (the voice of the Prime Minister) and Separatism (the leader of the terrorist organization) confront each other in the Gravel living room, no longer a place of peace and togetherness, but of division and strife. The father's moment of glory (a call from the Prime Minister) represents to the son a moment of betrayal (the denial of national pride, in speaking the other's language!) At the very moment the father sees his personal triumph at hand, the son appears in order to destroy this triumph. André's warning to his father, ''You have to refuse: you've no choice'' at first leaves everyone in stunned incomprehension. Eventually, O'Brien, in a frantic attempt to change the young man's mind involves André in a discussion of his political principles. Act One closes, and Act Two opens, on this battle of words.

On the surface, the second part of the play appears as a rather amorphous sequence of arguments between André and his elders. But this impression is deceptive. Careful analysis will show that the organization of Act Two is carried out most carefully, following a regular structural pattern of impeccable logic.

The entire second act—except for the brief final scene—consists of a verbal battle, organized into three rounds of increasing emotional impact and widening universal significance. The first round remains on the level of political theory. It consists of a long line of arguments brought forth by the older generation, (Pierre Gravel, Paul O'Brien), on the attack, with the younger generation (André) clearly on the defensive. The second stage of the battle is dominated by the figure of the mother, who brings the conflict from the political to the personal level. Emotionally, this is the core of the play. There are neither winners nor losers in this central round of the fight, only human beings sick at heart over the sufferings they must inflict on the ones they love most. In round three, the original situation is reversed: it is now the young generation (André and Nicole) who proceed to the attack, with the older generation on the defensive. This final round goes beyond the political issues to the universal problem of the differences in outlook between the generations, and its outcome is determined from the start: by the sheer logic of history, the older generation must make way for the new. Thus the structure of this act leads us imperceptibly from the particular (Federalism vs. Separatism) to the universal (the old generation making way for the new), setting the particular tragedy of the Canadian nation at a particular moment of its history into the universal context of the tragedy of the human situation, where no amount of love or goodwill can bridge the gap between succeeding generations. By setting the conflict in a family as united as the Gravels, Gélinas underlines the tragic inevitability of a conflict which is caused by forces outside the control of the protagonists, and which is a natural part of the human condition. The first round of argument centers around the traditional theoretical issues of federalism vs. separatism. Gravel and O'Brien alternately bring up their arguments, which are in turn deflected, if not invalidated, by André. Gélinas has been accused by some critics of oversimplification in the development of his argumentation in this particular part of the play. In his defence, one might say that a theatrical performance is scarcely the vehicle for overly sophisticated theoretical debate; nor can we expect it from an author whose often-stated purpose is to create a ''popular'' theatre capable of appealing to a common denominator. Quite apart from Gélinas' dramatic principles, one could say that the issues of the separatist debate were bound to turn eventually into a series of clichés, clichés which are nonetheless being taken very seriously by their proponents.

The arguments used by the older men are of course predictable: violence has been used before, and found wanting; the validity of the cause does not make an illegal act less unlawful; the aims of the nationalists could be more easily achieved by lawful means; isolating Quebec from the rest of Canada would be a regressive measure; and finally, the economic impossibility of a national state of Quebec. André counters each of these arguments. Of his statements, the most dramatically effective is his assurance that the new terrorism will cause no loss of life, and thus cannot be termed ''violence'' in the old sense of that word. Every precaution has been taken to limit the damage done by the bombs to buildings and monuments. This special aspect of André's terrorism serves to further increase the appeal of the character for the audience; the conflict can no longer be interpreted as ruthless violence against the forces of law and order; it is presented as a true conflict of ideologies. The totally idealistic quality of André's devotion to the cause, and his youthful optimism, further soften the negative connotation of his ''terrorist'' attitudes. André sincerely believes in the final triumph of Justice: ''Justice always wins in the end.'' His idealism is fully convincing. It is not simply the natural idealism of the young, but an idealism nurtured by the highly emotional nationalistic literature produced at the time. The attitude of the fictional André Gravel reflects clearly the writing of contemporary radicals like Chaput and Vallières — one must imagine André intoxicated by passages such as this one, from Vallières: ''I think there is no dream of mankind that cannot be realized . . . . I believe that man possesses the capacity to make an ever more human world and that there are no limits to the progress of humanity. I believe that revolution is possible and at the present stage of humanity logically necessary.''[3]

With the appearance of the mother in the next scene (Scene 7), the tone of the play changes radically from that of a heated, but still theoretical, debate to one of undisguised emotion. The generations find themselves confronting each other not on the political issues, not as federalists and separatists but simply now as old versus young. The political play now becomes both personal and universal, as the author brings out the deep affection of the members of the family for each other — affection fully counterbalanced by their irreconcilable views. André is visibly moved by the suffering he must inflict on his parents, especially his mother. Yet, he cannot do otherwise. As he explains in a lengthy letter (a somewhat clumsy dramatic device), the very self-reliance and honesty to himself which his mother has instilled into him throughout his childhood and adolescence demand that he should now act as he does. It is clear that the mother, who loves the two men equally, must make a choice. Louise pleads with André to spare his father, but has no ready answer for André's counter-arguments: "If I couldn't give in without destroying myself, what should I do, according to you . . . "; and, seeing her hesitation, he pushes on further: "Mother, answer me: between a belated career in politics for him, and something that's the whole meaning of life for me, which would you sacrifice?"

The presence of the mother has thus acted as a catalyst putting the problem into the context of a generation conflict. The moment André has formulated his position from this point of view, he is able to proceed to the attack, with the self-confidence of the young who cannot but win in the end: "The issue dividing the two of us, mother, has to do with the future, not the past. It has to do with building what's going to be our world: don't you understand! The world where Nicole and I and the rest of our generation will have to live, long after his generation . . . has gone with the wind . . . " The political issues which divide them have now become the mere symbols of an age-old situation, the struggle between the generations. André clearly sees the fight as a war, "and the next offensive will be launched by the young, . . . against the old". Pierre Gravel tries to fight back with the traditional catchwords at the disposal of an older generation on the defensive: "Experience, Logic and Reason versus Recklessness, Conceit and Ignorance — ". But André does not lack slogans with which to return the compliment, and he hurls at his father the stock insults of his generation for their elders: hypocrisy, unquestioning and unrealistic evaluation of the historical situation, lack of pride and idealism. The battle between father and son is on with all the elemental force which has characterized this primal situation ever since young Zeus overthrew his father Chronos, who had overthrown his parents Uranos and Ge to take over the reign of the universe.

Unable to win by logic, Pierre makes some last desperate attempts to turn André away from his chosen path by frightening him with a mention of police brutality and the horrors of imprisonment; but André is unimpressed. In the final round of the battle, Nicole joins forces with André. In an impassioned attack on the parents, she makes clear to them the full extent of the gap between them and their son: they simply do not speak the same language. Their attitudes are different to the point where communication is no longer possible — another cliché, but a cliché which takes on persuasive power in this particular context. Nicole is boiling, but her excesses are the excesses of the very young, carried away by a cause. She is almost comically patronizing towards Louise, whom she has always admired: "I don't hold any of the things you said earlier against you; you're enough of a woman to know your place is at your husband's side, even if among his numerous qualities he's as old-fashioned and as one-track-minded as a pre-war trolley!". In her total loyalty to André and his cause, however, Nicole becomes an admirable figure: "Now I'll lift (my head) proudly and tell everyone who wants to know: 'I am the fiancée of André Gravel, the political prisoner'. And when he comes out, if he still wants me, body and soul and everything else, I'll be waiting for him at the door with my suitcase . . . When I'm forty, I won't have to get a psychiatrist to give me a reason for living: I'll have one!" This final outburst by Nicole gives André the strength to act. Together, the two young people have won their battle. The old generation has gone down to defeat — as it must.

The dénouement in the brief final scene brings together all the strands of the action in a way which greatly intensifies the dramatic effect. Louise persuades her husband that in spite of everything that has happened, he must go on as planned, and deliver his scheduled speech in Toronto the next day. André and Nicole cross the room on their way to the police station just as Gravel dictates the emotion-packed final sentences of this speech to his secretary. A handshake between father and son silently testifies to the enduring love, as well as the irreconcilable differences, between the two men.

Hier les enfants dansaient was first performed at the Comédie Canadienne in April 1966[5] and in an English translation by Mavor Moore at the Centennial celebrations of the Charlottetown Festival in 1967. In 1968, the play was broadcast over the transcontinental network of the CBC, in 1971, over the educational networks of the United States. It was produced at the Théâtre de la Renaissance, Paris, in 1971.

The English version does not suffer from the same weaknesses as do those of *Tit-Coq* and *Bousille*; it does full justice to the original. This is due not only to the talent of the translator, but also to a large extent to the different quality of the play: set in an upper-middle-class milieu, and devoted largely to theoretical argumentation, this play can be transposed more easily into the language of another culture than can the more localized works of Gélinas.

Initial critical reaction to the play, in French as well as in English, suffered from the inability to view *Yesterday the Children Were Dancing* from a wider perspective than that of its topicality. This applies to both negative and positive criticism, with most of the negative criticism coming from the French side. Gélinas was accused of opportunism in his choice of subject matter, and, worse, of having created typically bourgeois, rather than revolutionary, theatre.[6] This attitude persists. In his *Le nouveau théâtre québecois*, 1973, Michel Bélair gives Gélinas the credit for having been the first to bring to the stage "the political problem which is rending Quebec society" but then he goes on to condemn the author (along with Marcel Dubé, Francoise Loranger, Jaques Ferron and Jaques Languirand!) for their "preoccupation with the universal"![7] Universality branded as a defect in a work of literature — an argument one could well imagine in the mouth of André Gravel!

Anglophone critics, on the other hand, hailed the play as a breakthrough in communication between the French and English communities of Canada, a feat of artistic consciousness-raising unequalled in the history of Canadian theatre: "At last, . . . a play that deals directly and forthrightly with the central fact of the Canadian conscience . . . a play which disturbs, unsettles and amuses, and vaults to an extraordinary level of political insight . . . . "[8]

Few critics on either side realized that besides having given voice to the agonies of a national crisis, Gélinas had also written a play of universal value and interest, a father-and-son drama which will likely be remembered when the separatist issue, like the nihilist ideology which inspired Turgenev, has become research material for historians.

Notes to Chapter Six

1. Pelletier, Gérard, *La Presse*, Nov. 18, 1961.

2. Chaput, Marcel, "Pourquoi je suis un séparatiste", in Scott, F. & Oliver, Michael, *Quebec States Her Case*, (Toronto, 1964), pp. 48-42.

3. After the death of his first wife in 1967, Gélinas married Huguette Oligny, a well-known actress who had been working with him since the days of *Tit-Coq*.

4. Valières, Pierre, *The White Niggers of America*, (Toronto, 1971), p. 230.

5. The première performance was directed by the author, with the following cast:
Pierre Gravel, Yves Létourneau
Paul O'Brien, Pierre Boucher
Raoul Roberge, Jean Lajeunesse
Larry Gravel, Alain Gélinas
Berthe Leroux, Marthe Nadeau
 (this character does not appear in the published versions of the play)
Nicole Chartier, Suzanne Lévesque
André Gravel, Yves Gélinas
Louise Gravel, Gisèle Schmidt

6. Basile, Jean, *Le Devoir*, April 13, 1966.

7. Bélair, Michel, op. cit. p. 36.

8. Cohen, Nathan, *Toronto Daily Star*, April 15, 1966.

BIBLIOGRAPHY

Gratien Gélinas

Plays:

French

Tit-Coq. Montreal: Beauchemin, 1950.

Bousille et les Justes. Quebec, Institut Littéraire du Québec, 1960.

Hier les enfants dansaient. Collection Théâtre Canadien, Montreal: Leméac, 1968.

English

Tit-Coq. Trans. Kenneth Johnstone in cooperation with the author. Toronto: Clarke Irwin, 1967.

Bousille and the Just. Trans. Kenneth Johnstone and Joffre Milville-Dechêne, Toronto: Clarke Irwin, 1961.

Yesterday the Children Were Dancing. Trans. Mavor Moore, Toronto: Clarke Irwin, 1967.

Articles and Speeches:

"Pour un théâtre national et populaire" — speech given on the occasion of receiving an honorary doctorate from the University of Montreal, Jan. 31, 1949; published in *Action Universitaire*, April, 1949.

"Why Broadway Turned Me Down." *Saturday Night*, March 6, 1951.

"Discrimination and Canada's Future." *Labour Gazette*, March 1955.

"Credo of the Comédie Canadienne." *Queen's Quarterly*, LXVI, Spring 1959.

"Jeune auteur, mon camarade". *Revue Dominicaine*, November 1960.

Selected Criticism on Gratien Gelinas

French

d'Auteuil, Georges Henri, S.J. "Bousille." *Relations*, October 1959.

d'Auteuil, Georges Henri, S.J. "Hier les enfants dansaient." *Relations*, June 1966.

Bobet, Jaques. "Bousille et les Justes." *Liberté* (November-December, 1959.)

Cartta, René-Salvator. "Tit-Coq au cinéma." *Relations*, April 1953.

Désrosiers, Pierre. "La nouvelle dramaturgie québecoise." *Culture Vivante*, V, 1967.

Duhamel, Roger. "Notre grand Fridolin." *Relations*, (May, 1945.)

Gélinas, Jean-Paul. "Bousille et les justes (1959-1969), de Gratien Gélinas." *Culture*, XXX, 3 (Sept. 1969.)

Gélinas, Marc. "Orientations de la dramaturgie nouvelle." *Culture Vivante*, no. 9, 1968.

Gagnon, Ernest, S.J. "Tit-Coq." *Relations*, (November, 1948.)

Hébert, Paul. "Entrevue." *Nord*, no. 4, 1973.

Laurendeau, Arthur. "Pour la 150 ième de Tit-Coq." *Action Nationale*, March/April 1949.

Laurendeau, Arthur. "Pour la 150ième de Tit-Coq." *Action Nationale*, Laurent, Edouard. "Réflexions sur le théâtre." *Culture*, March, 1945.

Laurent, Edouard. "Tit-Coq, un conscrit qui passera à l'histoire." *Culture*, Dec. 1948.

'La Barre du Jour, I, nos. 3, 4, 5, 1965. (Special theatre issue)

Toupin, Paul. "Fridolinons '45." *Amérique française*, March 1945.

English

Cohen, Nathan. "Theatre Today: English Canada." *Tamarack Review*, Autumn 1959.

Coulter, John. "Review of Fridolinons '46." *Saturday Night*, Jan. 18, 1947.

Cox, C. "Fridolin, the Bright French Star that Canada has 'Discovered'." *Saturday Night*, April 14, 1945.

Hamelin, Jean. "Theatre Today: French Canada." *Tamarack Review*, Autumn 1959.

Johnstone, K. "Fridolin . . . + Gratien Gélinas = Two Way Success." *Canadian Business*, March 1950.

Lefolii, K. "Interview with Gratien Gélinas." *MacLean's Magazine*, Jan. 30, 1960.

Michener, Wendy. "Toward a Popular Theatre." *Tamarack Review*, 13, Autumn 1959.

Ness, Margaret. "Little Rooster Flies the Coop." *Saturday Night*, Nov. 28, 1950.

Robertson, G. H. "Riches for the Little Rooster." *MacLean's Magazine*, Nov. 15, 1950.

Taaffe, J. "Gratien and the Terrorists." *MacLean's Magazine*, July 2, 1966.

CHRONOLOGY

1909	Gratien Gélinas born in Saint-Tite, Quebec
1915-1929	Schooling in Montreal; active in school drama societies.
1929	Leaves Collège de Montréal, where he had been pursuing classical studies.
1929-1937	Works for insurance company, La Sauvegarde; active in amateur theatricals and as monologue artist.
1932	Radio début in Robert Choquette's serial, "Le curé du village."
1937	"Fridolin" radio shows begin.
1937-1941	Weekly "Fridolin" show on radio CKAC, Montreal.
1938-1946	"Fridolinons," annual revue at the Monument National theatre
1946	Gélinas stars in "St. Lazare's Pharmacy", by Miklos Laszlo, in Montreal and Chicago.
1948	Première of *Tit-Coq*.
1949	Honorary doctorate from the University of Montreal.
1951	Honorary doctorate from the University of Toronto.
1953	Gélinas stars in film version of *Tit-Coq*.
1954	Gélinas stars in weekly television comedy written by himself, "Les Quat' Fers en L'Air" (CBC).
1956	"Fridolinons 56"
	Gélinas stars in *Henry V* and *The Merry Wives of Windsor* at Stratford.
1957-1963	Gélinas serves as Vice-President of the Greater Montreal Arts Council.
1958	Founding of the Comédie Canadienne.
	Gélinas is elected President of the Canadian Theatre Center.
1959	Première of *Bousille et les Justes*.
	Gélinas is made a member of the Royal Society.
1960	Gélinas becomes a founding member of the National Theatre School of Canada.
1964	Satirical revue, "Le Diable à Quatre", at the Comédie Canadienne.
1966	Premiére of *Hier, les enfants dansaient*.
1967	*Yesterday the Children Were Dancing* at the Charlottetown Festival.
	Gélinas is awarded the Grand Prix de Théâtre Victor Morin, by the Saint-Jean Baptiste Society; also, the Medal of the Order of Canada.
1969	Gélinas is named President of the Canadian Film Development Corporation.

Appendix

A National and Popular Theatre

Address delivered at the University of Montreal, January 31, 1949

Most Reverend Rector,
Honored Dean of the Faculty of Letters,
Ladies and Gentlemen,

At the end of a life filled with merit and good works, on the eve of giving an account to the Lord on the use of his numerous talents, the notary Jean-Baptiste Laframboise, main character of one of my sketches in "Fridolinons '45," found himself honored by the supreme distinction of having conferred upon him a doctorate *honoris causa* from the University of Montreal.

It may have been the impact on my subconscious of this part which I have played so often: on learning that a similar distinction was about to be awarded to me, to me who still considered myself in the green and growing stage of my career, I felt the slightly melancholy blush of a prematurely ripe fruit appearing on my brow. But I quickly recovered my composure by reasoning as follows:

In order to set an example, society sometimes admits the necessity of punishing a criminal much more severely than he would strictly speaking deserve. He pays a bit for his own misdeeds, of course, but especially for those of other criminals of his kind who are not on hand and who are to be inspired with a healthy fear.

That, I said to myself, is exactly what is happening today, with this difference, that the criminal is what they call a dramatic author, that the punishment is turned into a reward and that the healthy fear becomes a stimulant. Nevertheless, it remains the perfect scapegoat situation.

Let me stress this very much: the honor of which you have made me the recipient tonight, I accept less in my own name than in the name of those who have cleared the land where we are now able to reap a harvest. I share this award with all those authors who, with varying success, but animated by the same love of the stage and the same faith in our national future, have worked and are still working for the establishment, *chez nous*, of an indigenous form of theatrical expression.

There will be some who will be surprised at this official recognition which you are bestowing, through me, on dramatic art.

Ever since the medieval period, when jugglers and mountebanks shared with the highway robbers and lepers the disdain of respectable people — ever since the time, less than fifty years after the death of Shakespeare, when the British parliament ordered the theatres closed and had actors tied to a cart and whipped, — ever since that sad night when the remains of the great Molière were refused interment in sacred ground, the theatre has suffered too much opprobrium to be concerned over a last remnant of scorn which may still affect some reaction minds.

One of my sons, the one among the five who was then eight years old, asked me one day at the dinner table, between a pear and a piece of Oka cheese:

"Papa, a thaumaturge, is that a gentleman who makes plays for the theatre?"

"No," I answered, "not necessarily. A gentleman who writes plays is called a 'dramaturge'. A thaumaturge is a holy man who works miracles."

He said: "So, thaumaturge and dramaturge — "

"Yes, they rhyme, that's all. Do you know what a miracle is?"

Oh yes. As far as miracles were concerned, he was well informed. He even recited for me, almost word for word, the definition of "miracle" given in the "Annotated Cathechism for the Ecclesiastical Provinces of Quebec, Montreal and Ottawa", in the middle of page 40.

But the definition of a stage play was somewhat beyond him.

This incident set me thinking. The situation was serious if a child of eight, whose mental age corresponds, as they say (no doubt erroneously) to the mental age of the average public, if a child of eight, as I said, could have the impudence of confusing in such a way God's intervention with man's invention.

And I decided that I must do something in order to prove to my son that a dramatist has nothing in common with a thaumaturge and that the composition of a dramatic work is not of a miraculous nature.

This was perhaps one of the reasons why I wrote *Tit-Coq*.

I have written this play for another, and infinitely more serious, reason.

It happened that one day I read the following lines in the first act of *L'Echange*, of Claudel: "Man is bored and ignorance is part of him from birth. And not knowing of anything how it begins or ends, this is why he goes to the theatre. And he looks at himself, his hands in his lap. And he laughs and he cries, and he does not feel like going away."

I read these lines twenty times over: *"man is bored . . . this is why he goes to the theatre; and he looks at himself, his hands in his lap; and he laughs and he cries, and he does not feel like going away."*

And I thought about our audiences, our Canadian audiences which have been accused for decades of all the sins of the theatre, and which have been called indifferent, stupid or ignorant each time a production did not achieve the success which was expected. Less and less, this audience was laughing in the theatre; less and less, it was crying; more and more, it did feel like going away; it hardly even felt like coming at all any more. And I asked myself if the explanation for this phenomenon was not all there, in the lines of Claudel.

Did our public really see <u>itself</u> in the theatre? Instead of a reflection of itself, was it not rather offered the portrait of another, even if this other one was a cousin, even if the painting was often well done and the framing in the best of taste?

Given an opportunity to see itself, and not another, in the theatre, maybe this good audience would laugh, maybe it would cry, its hands in its lap, maybe it wouldn't feel like going away.

Maybe. The theory still had to be tested. To be tested by plays where our public would see itself as much as possible. It was well worth trying, of that I was sure.

But before devoting my life to the propagation of this faith, I decided that I had to give it a solid foundation in my own mind through logical reasoning.

Which is exactly what I have done, arriving at the conclusion that *the purest form of dramatic art* — I do not say the only one but the purest — *would be the one which represents as closely as possible that same audience to which this theatre addresses itself.*

And I will try to demonstrate to you that I am right, by using an example which everyone — or nearly everyone — can understand: marriage.

Any old maid will tell you, with more or less bitterness, that it takes two to make a marriage—a man and a woman, to be exact—and that these two parties must necessarily unite.

Theatre, then, is the marriage of two essential elements, indispensable to each other: the stage and the audience.

In his *Art of the Theatre*, Ghéon says: "Dramatic art is neither an author who composes a play somewhere in a corner, nor even a company of trained actors who bring it to life on a stage; it is also an audience which must receive it. It is, on the one hand, an author and his actors, on the other, an audience. It would be useless to attempt to do away with one of those two elements: they are complementary. One might conceive of a painting which a painter would do only to please himself. One might conceive of a poem which a poet would recite to himself from morning till night, and keep from the rest of mankind. One might conceive of a novel which would never be read and rest forever in its box. But it is impossible to conceive of a dramatic work which, once written, rehearsed, and produced, would take place in front of empty seats—or at least, if it should happen, it would be much against the intentions of the actors and the author: its end does not lie there."

Thus, for theatre to come to be, two elements are necessary, the stage and the audience. And I would add that these two elements must not only come together in one building, but that they must also unite, melt into each other to live jointly the same drama.

It is Giraudoux who has said, in *L'Impromptu de Paris*: "If the entire audience, once the lights have gone out, is there, all tense and rapt, it is because it wishes to lose itself, to give itself, to abandon itself. If the actor is there on the stage, in the wings, tense and rapt, ready to enter into the luminous trap of the setting, it is because he, too, wishes to lose himself, to give himself, to abandon himself."

And Jouvet for his part states, in his *Reflections of an Actor*: "The theatre exists only in the moment of theatre, this unique moment where the participants —actors, authors and spectators—carried away, taken out of themselves, melt and dissolve slowly into each other, in the moment when the audience and the stage are coupled and fused to each other by the peripeties of the play."

It is obvious: if the public does not espouse the conflict which takes place on stage, there is no theatre, there is only a facsimile of theatre. Just as marriage will exist in name only if the spouses are simply together under one roof, but not united in flesh and in spirit.

Now, if we must admit, with Jouvet and Giraudoux, that this total communion between the audience and the stage is the very essence of dramatic art, we must by that very fact realize that anything which provides an obstacle to such a union, or reduces its perfection, is hostile to the principle of theatre.

In our own theatres, how can such a perfect communion — a communion which, I repeat, is indispensable — be achieved between our own public and a playwright of a foreign mentality?

Jacques Copeau said the following: "True theatre will be possible only when the man in the audience will be able to whisper the words together with the man on stage, at the same time and in the same spirit."

How can a Canadian in the audience whisper, at the same time and in the same spirit, the words of a foreign author, even if this author should be French?

For, in the theatre no more than elsewhere, can we count on France to represent us. I am not saying this, these are the words of Etienne Gilson:

"It is certain," he wrote recently in the periodical *Une Semaine dans le Monde*, "that Canada, where French is spoken, is not France. The close affinity of the languages presents for the observer the source of an illusion which, though difficult to avoid, remains nonetheless an illusion. When a Canadian speaks or writes in French, he is the spokesman of a people whose history is not our history, and whose life differs from ours as radically as his landscape differs from that of the country where we live."

"Officially separated for two centuries, with differences that go back even further, the Frenchman and the Canadian have neither the same past nor the same future. Therefore, they do not share a same present, a same continuity, a same life, a same mode of being. And this is why, even though they use the same language, they create two distinct literatures, each of which may benefit from the techniques of the other one, but which spring from two different sources.''

Thus, if the act of theatre necessitates that actor and spectator melt and dissolve into each other, with the man in the audience *seeing himself* and whispering the words together with the man on stage, *in the same spirit and at the same time*, this union will never be as total, at least in principle, as in the case of an author and a public who share *the same essence, the same stock, the same past, the same present and the same future*.

And I maintain that, given not only an equal, but even a vastly inferior dramatic quality in comparison with the great masterpieces of the foreign theatre, past or present, a play of Canadian inspiration and expression will always appeal more to our public.

I have verified the truth of this disturbing phenomenon, which may seem incorrect at first sight, by passing from theory to practice.

I do not intend here to deny fully the appeal of a foreign theatre. An audience which does not see itself reflected in it will be able to appreciate it, but for reasons which are less pure and essential, which will be based, e.g., on novelty, exoticism or literary qualities.

Which comes back to affirming that, contrary to music and painting, theatre will always be first and foremost a national endeavor, since it is necessarily limited by its language. If, accidentally, because of its human or dramatic transcendence, it should reach the universal, a translation, even the most faithful one, will always rob it of some of its intrinsic value. Listen to a Mozart symphony, and you will be sure that you can enjoy it as much as a German or a Frenchman. But you will always miss out on something if you do not hear in his original language even the most universal of dramatists, Shakespeare.

In a lecture on *Hamlet* which he had just produced in Paris in an adaptation by Gide, Jean-Louis Barrault recently made this candid reflection: ''Whatever the beauty of Gide's translation, it seems that in English, it is even more profound.''

And Ghéon states: ''Neither Aeschylus, nor Shakespeare, nor Sophocles nor Calderon have written their dramas to be read, but for the stage, and a specific stage, for a public and a specific public, for an immediate, and, let us admit it, ephemeral realization. At a distance of several hundred years, in spite of a clear tradition and incontestable documentation, we cannot even imagine how Mmes. Champmeslé or DuParc interpreted Racine. The cleverest reconstructions which we are presented with on stage remain transpositions. What connection can there possibly be between the original *Antigone* of the Theatre of Dionysos, and the academic *Antigone* of the Comédie Française, even at the time when Mounet-Sully and Julia Bartet gave it all of their inspired genius? What the real *Antigone* was like we shall never know, nor the *Passion of Gréban, Othello, Phaedra* or the *Misanthrope*. From the combined effort of those who conceived and animated these productions, we have nothing left but the text, the skeleton, the concentrate, admirable no doubt, which the books have transmitted to us. Having become the material of which classics are made, material for analysis in textbooks and classrooms, and matter for the secret enjoyment of a lettered élite, this theatre has become literature.''

It is therefore easy for me to claim that in the theatre even the classics belong only in a relative sense to all periods and all countries and that a people cannot count on them to express its age and its genius.

Ghéon has just said it: classical theatre, secret enjoyment of a lettered élite. It is true that the higher one rises, the wider the panorama becomes. But let us not forget that the theatre, an essentially collective art form, is made for men and not only for supermen.

Do not misunderstand me. I do not wish to see foreign dramatic works and especially the French theatre banished from our stages. Not at all. Because a man who wishes to see himself needs mirrors in his house, he would be wrong in relegating to the attic all the portraits of his family.

In the intimate family of our national theatre, we shall always be happy to welcome with open arms the most charming and attractive among our French cousins.

This need for independence is a purely theatrical one which has nothing to do with political nationalism and it would be most unfair to interpret it as an outburst of francophobia.

We are of French descent, it is true, and it is in the French genius that our collective personality has found its most evident character traits, but we cannot be accused of ingratitude if we now wish to live our own intellectual lives, according to our own aptitudes and means. Even though he has been for a while part of her who has given him birth, even though, for a long time, he has been able to live and breathe only through her and with her, the son who has become an adult now has the right to leave his mother's apron strings—though she may be the most beautiful, the most intelligent and the most cultured of mothers.

I then sum up the first part of the thesis I have just been exposing to you, in simple terms, at the risk of being considered a *terroir* writer:

— Theatre is the marriage of two essential elements: the stage and the audience.
— In order to be fully consummated, marriage requires not only the coming together of the constituent parties, but also their total union.
—Therefore, audience and stage must necessarily melt into each other in order for the principle of the theatre to be realized.

From which I deduce that the author and his actors on the one hand, and the audience on the other, must, in order for this perfect communion to take place, be preferably of the same essence, since it is known that mixed marriages are usually more difficult than others to conduct successfully.

Furthermore, if it is true, to repeat Jouvet, that "the theatre exists only in this unique moment where the participants—actors and spectators—carried away, taken out of themselves, melt and dissolve into each other, in the moment when the audience and the stage are coupled and fused to each other by the peripeties of the play" it is by the same token true that the actor and the audience must forget as much as possible that they are on a stage or in the auditorium of a theatre. And I conclude that the best constructed play is the one which makes us forget that it is well constructed; that the best staging is the one of which the spectator does not become fully conscious, so natural and inevitable it seems; and that the best actor is the one who makes us forget how well he acts so that we become interested only in the character he impersonates.

"It is a great art to hide art", as Boileau has said.

This first part of my thesis having established that <u>a theatre must be first and foremost national</u>, I shall now try to demonstrate briefly that <u>its principle requires further that it should be popular in nature</u>.

I have just said that the theatre is an art form whose joys are essentially collective. I can very well imagine you, all by yourself in your living room, becoming enthused over the reading of a poem or listening to a symphony, but I cannot at all visualize you, solitary spectator in an empty theatre, throwing your program up into the air in a delirium of enthusiasm, after the curtain has fallen on a dramatic masterpiece.

The audience being thus an essentially collective unit, which must, in spirit, ascend to the stage to "lose, give and abandon" itself so that there should be a real theatrical experience, the ideal dramatic form must therefore be the one which will interest the audience in its totality, the one which will reach not only the most numerous, but also the most diversified public.

The dramatist facing an audience finds himself, in my opinion, in the same situation as a student of mathematics whose professor has asked him to find the common denominator of a series lined up on the blackboard. For the dramatic author, this common denominator means the heart of his spectators, for it is a fact that just about everybody carries a heart in his bosom, but very few people have a head on their shoulders. And if the conflict of two opposing passions can be understood by all, it is only a minority who will be able to follow the logical development of a reasoning process.

In the theatre, where the word is king, one reaches the heart mainly by passing through the ears. "The dramatic author," to quote Ghéon once again, "must make sure that he does not speak a language different from that of his audience. Even if it is rich in meanings and overflowing with imagery, the language he uses must be common to all. What is the use of finding the precise word, the correctly constructed phrase, if the idea which he exposes or the feeling he expresses finds no correspondence in the thoughts and the hearts of his audience."

Furthermore, John Addington Symmons has said, in referring to the Elizabethan period, certainly the most glorious one in the history of the English theatre: ''The reason why dramatic art reached such heights at the time was that the authors lived and wrote in full accord with the people as a whole.''

A playwright who would be reproached with using an overly popular dramatic idiom would therefore have the right to reply, if this language fits his characters and if these characters really belong to his people: ''Change the language of the public and my text will automatically change in the same direction. Otherwise, how could the man in the audience, as Copeau demands, ''whisper the same words together with the man on stage, at the same time and in the same spirit?''

Besides, does it not make sense that in our theatreless society the taste for things dramatic should be acquired first through a popular form, capable of attracting every public and of uniting in one and the same emotion the great and the humble, the rich and the poor, the ignorant and the learned?

And when this imposing cathedral of the theatre will have been erected, others will then be able to come and build inside its walls any number of chapels where the devotees will separate from the ordinary crowd after the great common dramatic service, and kneel down in the niche of their choice to worship at their ease divine poetry, holy literature, venerable philosophy, or simply drop their offering in the almsbox of blessed vulgarity.

What interests me about this splendid edifice is the construction itself; it is the rough work of the mason, who must first lay the foundations, but who fully intends, if God grants him life and strength, to rise slowly as stone after stone is passed from one mason to the next, fully conscious of the fact that the lines of the temple he is helping to build will have to lose some of their heaviness and gain refinement as they rise towards the heavens.

If ever I should abandon this task for another one which might appear more glorious, I would no longer dare feel proud of the distinction you have so generously conferred on me tonight.

Gratien Gélinas

Index